THE JOLT EFFECT

THE
JOLT
EFFECT

HOW HIGH

PERFORMERS

OVERCOME

CUSTOMER

INDECISION

Matthew Dixon and **Ted McKenna**

PORTFOLIO / PENGUIN

PORTFOLIO / PENGUIN
An imprint of Penguin Random House LLC
penguinrandomhouse.com

Most Portfolio books are available at a discount when purchased in
quantity for sales promotions or corporate use. Special editions, which
include personalized covers, excerpts, and corporate imprints, can be created
when purchased in large quantities. For more information, please call
(212) 572-2232 or e-mail specialmarkets@penguinrandomhouse.com.
Your local bookstore can also assist with discounted bulk purchases using
the Penguin Random House corporate Business-to-Business program.
For assistance in locating a participating retailer,
e-mail B2B@penguinrandomhouse.com.

Graphics by Tethr.

Library of Congress Cataloging-in-Publication Data

Names: Dixon, Matthew, 1972- author. | McKenna, Ted (Business consultant), author.
Title: The jolt effect : how high performers overcome customer indecision /
Matthew Dixon and Ted McKenna.
Description: New York : Portfolio/Penguin, [2022] |
Includes bibliographical references and index.
Identifiers: LCCN 2022013122 (print) | LCCN 2022013123 (ebook) |
ISBN 9780593538104 (hardcover) | ISBN 9780593538111 (ebook)
Subjects: LCSH: Consumer behavior. | Decision making. | Customer relations. | Selling.
Classification: LCC HF5415.32 .D58 2022 (print) | LCC HF5415.32 (ebook) |
DDC 658.8/342—dc23/eng/20220601
LC record available at https://lccn.loc.gov/2022013122
LC ebook record available at https://lccn.loc.gov/2022013123

Printed in the United States of America
1st Printing

BOOK DESIGN BY TANYA MAIBORODA

Matt wishes to thank his wife, Amy,
and his kids, Aidan, Ethan, Norah, and Clara—
all of whom find it supremely ironic and endlessly amusing
that he wrote a book about how to overcome indecision.

Ted would like to thank his wife, Alison,
and kids, Will and Ella, for the support and love.
You'll now have an easier answer to the question
"What is it you do, again?"

The burdens that make us groan and sweat,
The troubles that make us fume and fret,
Are the things that haven't happened yet.

—GEORGE W. BAIN

CONTENTS

PREFACE *xi*

INTRODUCTION *xiii*

CHAPTER 1
The Inaction Paradox *1*

CHAPTER 2
The JOLT Effect *32*

CHAPTER 3
Judge the Indecision *43*

CHAPTER 4
Offer Your Recommendation *72*

CHAPTER 5
Limit the Exploration *89*

CHAPTER 6

Take Risk Off the Table *111*

CHAPTER 7

Becoming a "Buyer's Agent" *130*

CHAPTER 8

Beyond Win Rates: JOLT-ing Customer Loyalty *145*

CHAPTER 9

How Much Is Indecision Costing You? *158*

CHAPTER 10

Applying JOLT in Different Sales Environments *178*

CHAPTER 11

Building the JOLT-Capable Sales Force *194*

ACKNOWLEDGMENTS *207*

NOTES *211*

INDEX *219*

A Unique Moment in Time

If there's one study that is the envy of every sales researcher, it's the groundbreaking work done by Professor Neil Rackham and his team, as profiled in the book *SPIN Selling*.[1] Twelve years to complete. Thirty-five thousand sales calls observed. One hundred and sixteen unique factors assessed for their potential impact on sales outcomes. More than one million dollars ($2.3 million in today's dollars) spent on the study. For more than thirty years, this study has been considered the gold standard of sales research. It was a study so broad, so deep, and so resource-intensive that nobody dared to even ask if it could be repeated, let alone surpassed.

It wasn't the number of calls studied or the number of variables in the study that was the challenge. Advances in big data analytics, machine learning, and GPU-powered processing have made it possible to study *much* larger data sets and to consider far more factors than Rackham's team had. The issue has always been that many sales conversations—especially the most pivotal ones—take place in the customer's office. Collecting the data therefore meant committing to traveling the world to actually sit in on those sales meetings and observe what was happening. No organization would sponsor a study like that given the cost, time, and resources required—and especially given the uncertain outcomes of such an undertaking.

But something interesting and altogether surprising happened in the spring of 2020. As the world went into lockdown due to the COVID-19 pandemic, all sales became virtual—literally overnight.

For sales researchers like ourselves, this represented a once-in-a-lifetime opportunity.

Partnering with several dozen companies, our research team went to work collecting *millions* of sales conversations recorded on platforms like Zoom, Teams, and Webex as well as the dozens of bespoke recording platforms used by companies all over the world. Using automatic speech recognition, we turned the unstructured audio from these recordings into unstructured text. Then, using a machine learning platform from a conversation intelligence company called Tethr, we brought structure to that data, tagging more than 8,300 unique factors across those sales calls. Finally, we did the math to determine which of these factors drive sales performance and which do not.

And what emerged from this analysis was a story that was entirely unexpected.

Stuck

For as long as sales training has been delivered and sales books have been written, there's been one singular objective we've all been focused on: How do we overcome the customer's status quo?

Focusing on the customer's status quo makes perfect sense. After all, it's a formidable enemy—one that salespeople lose to all the time. Human beings have a deep-seated bias for things to remain as they are. And customers, we all know, will regularly pass on pursuing opportunities that have been clearly demonstrated to make them better off.

It should come as no surprise, then, that companies have spent untold amounts of time and money on sales training, coaching, and enablement in order to help salespeople overcome the customer's status quo. Sales organizations equip their reps with better scripting, tighter value proposition messaging, customer case studies, reviews, testimonials, proof points, ROI calculators, and objection-handling techniques—all designed to help the customer get over the hump, to get them to say yes to their offers and no to doing more of the same.

Of course, there is no shortage of opinions as to how to do this. Some say it's about building trust while others argue it's about diagnosing needs. In fact, we wrote about this very problem in *The Challenger Sale* more than a decade ago. In that research, we discovered that the best sellers—Challengers—bring disruptive, provocative insights that reframe the customer's thinking as to how to make money, save money, or mitigate risk. What these gifted reps had figured out was that the way to get the customer to move forward is to show them that "the pain of same is worse than the pain of change."

But that is not what this book is about.

This book is about a newer, more nefarious, and seemingly intractable problem facing salespeople today: What happens when the customer agrees that the status quo is unacceptable, that yours is the only solution that can help them attain their objectives, that the whole buying committee is on board . . . and you *still* lose?

This sort of thing happens more often than you might think.

In our research, we found that anywhere between 40 percent and 60 percent of deals today end up stalled in "no decision" limbo. To be clear, these are customers who go through the *entire sales process*—consuming valuable seller time and organizational resources, perhaps even engaging in extended pilots or proof-of-concept trials—only to end up not crossing the finish line.

What is a salesperson to do in this situation—when they've overcome the customer's status quo, won the battle for competitive differentiation, gotten the customer to *say* they want their company's solution . . . and yet, they *still* don't buy? What playbook do they follow when their hard-fought deal ends up in the wasteland of inaction—when the sale ends not with a signature but with the customer saying they "still need to think about it"?

Our research shows that they do what they've been taught to do for years.

When customers balk and start to get cold feet, sellers tend to go back to the well. They assume it must be because they haven't successfully overcome the customer's status quo. Perhaps the customer doesn't fully appreciate the problem that their solution is designed to solve. Or maybe they don't yet see enough daylight between their company's solution and that of the competition. So, salespeople break out their arsenal of tools to prove to the customer the many ways their solutions will help them win. And, when push comes to shove, they dial up the FUD—or, fear, uncertainty, and doubt—to tap into the customer's fear of missing out. They show the customer what they stand to lose by not making this purchase today. They try to create a burning platform that the customer has no choice but to abandon.

And yet, our research also shows—in very stark terms—that none of this works. In fact, these time-honored sales tactics that have been passed on from leader to manager to seller for decades aren't just *unproductive*; they're actually *counterproductive* to the goal of getting the customer off the fence.

But why?

This is the question our research team spent more than a year trying to answer.

And in the process, we discovered something truly surprising. The status quo—which salespeople have always been taught is their biggest, if not only, enemy—actually isn't either of those things.

Our research reveals that losing to the status quo is actually one of *two* possible reasons a deal can be lost to inaction and is, in fact, the less menacing of the two. While the customer's preference for the status quo is, no doubt, a significant obstacle that every salesperson must overcome if they wish to sell anything, there is a second, more challenging obstacle that remains even after the status quo has been defeated: the customer's own inability to make a decision.

What makes customer indecision such a dangerous threat to salespeople?

First, indecision has a more powerful grip on the customer's mind than any preference they may have for the status quo. Preference for the status quo is driven by a set of human biases that, simply stated, lead customers to want things to remain as they are. Customer indecision, however, is driven by a separate and distinct psychological effect called the omission bias, which is the customer's desire to avoid making a mistake. And of the two, it is the omission bias that represents the more difficult obstacle for the salesperson to overcome. In fact, statistically speaking, customer indecision accounts for more of the deals lost to inaction than any preference for the status quo. Customers, it turns out, are much less worried about *missing out* than they are about *messing up*.

Second, indecision is extremely difficult for salespeople to detect. While customers are perfectly comfortable stating their preference for the status quo—that they believe the way they do things today is perfectly fine or that they don't see the vendor's solution as a more compelling alternative—the same cannot be said of indecision. Because it is driven by deeply personal fears, indecision is not something that customers openly discuss with salespeople. In fact, it's often something customers aren't even aware they're struggling with at all. Yet, our data shows that it is everywhere. Nearly 87 percent of sales opportunities contain either moderate or high levels of indecision. And it is toxic: as indecision increases, win rates plummet.

Third, the drivers of indecision are getting worse as the customer buying environment changes. The customer's preference for the status quo is a constant, monolithic obstacle in sales; it has gotten neither better nor worse with time. Customers today are just as likely to prefer the status quo as customers were twenty years ago or will be twenty years from now. But indecision has a set of discrete psychological drivers that are fueled by environmental factors beyond our control. As the number of options available to customers increases, as the amount of information available to research those options expands, and as the cost and risk of vendor solutions continues to rise, so too does the propensity for customers to become indecisive and, ultimately, do nothing.

The final reason that indecision poses such an enormous challenge to today's salesperson is perhaps the most troubling: salespeople themselves are unknowingly contributing to the problem. Because the conventional wisdom is that the status quo is the salesperson's biggest competitor, reps have only ever been sent into battle with one playbook. But overcoming indecision requires a fundamentally *different* approach from what is used to beat the status quo. Where overcoming the status quo is about dialing *up* the fear of *not* purchasing, overcoming indecision is about dialing *down* the fear *of* purchasing. And, if the wrong playbook is applied in a pursuit, our research shows that it can backfire dramatically. When sellers use the status quo playbook on a customer who is, in fact, struggling with indecision, they actually make the customer *more* indecisive, therefore increasing the odds that the deal will end up stalling out and dying on the vine. Yet, for the salesperson who has been taught to believe that their only real enemy is the status quo, that playbook becomes their hammer and every hesitant customer looks like a nail.

So how are sellers supposed to fight an enemy they've never been taught to recognize and never been equipped to defeat?

Here, we do what we have always done: we look to what star salespeople have already figured out on their own. Research over the years has shown that the best reps have a knack for figuring out new approaches to systemic problems when no playbook exists. They're gifted at adapting to new challenges and overcoming whatever stands in their way. Researchers often refer to this as the "lead steer effect": the leaders in the group change direction as they spot new obstacles and opportunities and the rest of the herd follows. So, if you want to know what everybody will be doing in the future, look to what the leaders are doing now.

Neil Rackham's seminal book *SPIN Selling* told the story of how top sellers had figured out how to sell more complex solutions to their customers, years before any sales organization was training its reps on solution-selling techniques. In *The Challenger Sale*, we explored how top performers deal with the problem of customers learning on their own, engaging sellers very late, and forcing them to compete on price—a problem that has only become worse in recent years. And in *The Challenger Customer*, we shared research on how the best reps navigate another obstacle confounding today's sellers: the propensity of customers to bring more and more stakeholders to the table to weigh in on a purchase decision.

Perhaps not surprisingly, high performers have also developed a playbook for overcoming customer indecision and winning this decisive aspect of the sale—despite never having been taught how to do so.

In a first-of-its-kind study, our research team used machine learning to study millions of sales conversations across industries. The result: a new playbook, based on *four unique behaviors* that high performers use for navigating and overcoming customer indecision. This isn't just a case of stars being stars, executing standard sales techniques at a higher level. Instead, many of these behaviors are actually contrary to the status quo playbook that has been taught and reinforced by sales trainers for years.

Together, they form a new playbook—which we call the JOLT method—that is purpose-built for overcoming customer indecision.

For sales leaders, managers, and reps, this is a problem absolutely worth solving. It's no overstatement to say that figuring out a way to overcome customer indecision—to close the gap between "I want" and "I did"—represents the single greatest opportunity to inflect growth for the average business.

Over the course of this book, we'll share with you our research regarding the impact of customer indecision on sales, the social science that explains why the status quo playbook backfires when used to combat indecision, the "flavors" of customer indecision salespeople will encounter in the market, the corresponding high-performer behaviors for overcoming them, and the guidance for how to implement the JOLT method in your own sales organization.

We hope you'll read on, that you'll be as surprised and encouraged by our findings as we were, and, most importantly, that you'll find a new pathway to greater levels of sales performance than you ever thought possible.

THE JOLT EFFECT

CHAPTER ONE

The Inaction Paradox

S ometimes the smallest event can change the whole course of a massive, planned undertaking in very unexpected ways.

This is exactly what happened to us.

Early on in our study—as the findings came pouring out of our machine learning platform and we were struggling to make sense of what they were telling us—we accepted an invitation to sit in on a pipeline review with a sales leader we'd known for years and whose sales instincts we deeply respected. This person had cut her teeth selling mainframe computers and networking equipment back in the day and today runs one of the largest and most successful sales organizations in the cloud computing industry.

The pipeline review started innocuously enough, but then something curious happened. An experienced rep who had forecast a big deal to close for the last two quarters—but had instead seen it continue to slip—was being grilled about the opportunity. The rep seemed to have done everything right. He'd taught the customer about an unseen opportunity that only the company's solution could address. He'd helped them execute a successful proof of concept that won over the technical users in the organization. He'd managed to convince a skeptical buying committee—proving the ROI of the solution and defending the company's unique differentiators and value proposition. His buyer told him that they were ready to move forward.

But then, suddenly, the deal went cold. Weeks turned into months and months into quarters. The customer went from frequent and robust conversations with the rep to offering only curt replies, often days after emails had been sent. In the last email the rep had received, the customer said, "Priorities here are shifting. We should probably pick this conversation up again next year." What had once seemed like a sure thing now seemed to be another deal about to be lost to inaction. The discussion in the pipeline review was whether to "kill for cause" or keep putting time and resources into pursuing it.

Then, the head of sales asked a question that took us all by surprise.

"Do you think the customer is committed to maintaining their status quo or just indecisive about changing it?" she asked.

"I'm not sure I follow," the rep replied. "What's the difference?"

"Actually, quite a lot," she said.

And just like that, our entire study took on new meaning. As soon as we hung up the phone, our team went to work, poring over the data to test her assertion.

From the very first pass through the data, it was clear that something very strange was going on in the sales calls we had collected—something we hadn't expected or even thought to look for before that pipeline review: *an overwhelming number of customers who said that they were ready to buy ended up as lost opportunities for the salesperson.*

The Real Enemy in Sales

There has always been a wide range of opinions about the best *way* to sell, but there has never been any disagreement that the customer's status quo is every salesperson's biggest competitor.

While there are plenty of other vendors and suppliers out there that a salesperson must contend with, they all pale in comparison to the threat posed by the customer's desire for things to remain as they are and their deep-seated aversion to change. For this reason, sales organizations have poured time and resources into equipping their salespeople to defeat the status quo. It's the focus of nearly every sales training session, coaching one-on-one, and pep talk delivered to sellers. It's the enemy that every piece of content—from messaging to case studies to proof points and ROI calculators—is focused on. It's no overstatement to say that beating the status quo has become the singular rallying cry for nearly every sales organization on earth.

It would therefore stand to reason that in sales, when a deal ends up stalling out, lost to inaction, the only possible explanation is that the salesperson has failed to break the gravitational pull of the customer's status quo.

And yet, this is not what we found.

When we look at all of the deals in our study that ended up marked as lost to "no decision," a completely different picture from the one that has been painted for salespeople emerges. While the customer's preference for the status quo is a big competitor, it is not the *only* reason a deal can end up lost in this way. Instead, we found that there is a second reason: the customer's own inability to make a decision. Or, put simply, *customer indecision* (see Figure 1.1).

But even more surprisingly, of these two drivers, it is indecision that accounts for *more* of these losses than the status quo. Across all of the deals we studied, we found that only 44 percent of deals that end up lost to inaction are due to the customer's preference for the status quo—either not believing that things are bad enough to change or not agreeing that the vendor's solution represents a more compelling alternative. But 56 percent of the time, the customer expresses a desire to abandon their status quo and move forward in a new way with the vendor's solution but, for one reason or another, is unwilling or unable to make a decision and commit (see sidebar "How We Did the Research").

For salespeople who have grown up being taught that the status quo is their biggest competitor, the idea that the customer's preference for the status quo accounts for *less than half* of losses

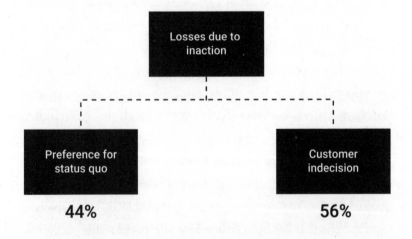

FIGURE 1.1: Breakdown of losses to inaction by root cause

due to inaction is as shocking as it is troubling. Readers are likely to ask the obvious question—How do we overcome customer indecision?—and, to be clear, this will be our focus for the rest of this book. But in order to appreciate the importance of overcoming indecision, we need to first understand how it differs, in fundamental ways, from a preference for the status quo.

HOW WE DID THE RESEARCH

To better understand how the best sellers combat indecision, our research team at Tethr, a conversation intelligence software company, used a combination of automatic speech recognition, natural language processing, and machine learning to study more than 2.5 million sales calls from dozens of companies across a variety of industries, representing both simple transactional sales (which were often inbound) and highly complex "solution sales" (which were largely outbound). It's worth briefly explaining how we did this research, as the idea of analyzing 2.5 million sales calls can seem unfathomable.

Working with our participant companies, we were able to collect large samples of recorded sales calls. Some of the companies in our study used platforms like Zoom, Teams, or Webex to record their sales calls. Others that operate in more traditional call center settings (e.g., inside sales groups) recorded calls centrally using a recording platform. Regardless of the format, we took the unstructured audio recordings these companies sent us and, using a transcription engine, converted them into unstructured text. Then, to bring structure to the data, we used a machine learning platform to identify when and where certain behaviors, actions, or "events" occurred in the calls. For example, we trained the platform to identify any situation in which a customer expressed price concern or when a rep diagnosed customer needs. Collectively, we taught the machine to identify several hundred such concepts.

Identifying nuanced concepts in unstructured text is complicated. Take, for instance, a customer expressing a concern or objection to the price of a vendor's offering. If you think about it, there are *hundreds* of possible ways a person could say "I think it's too expensive." The key is to train the machine to identify all of the phrases, utterances, and articulations that *could* be expressed and to teach it to tell the difference between an utterance that is an accurate reflection of price concern (e.g., "That's too rich for my blood!") and one that isn't (e.g., "Boy, that's rich coming from you!"). For several years, the team at Tethr has been working on honing the training set used by its machine learning platform in order to produce results that hit at an extremely high level of accuracy—effectively minimizing instances of false positives (i.e., when the machine says it's spotted a concept but, in fact, what it spotted isn't an accurate representation of that concept) and false negatives (i.e., when the machine missed a given concept because it was articulated in a way that it had not been trained to recognize). Without doing this, you end up with a "garbage in, garbage out" problem, the underlying data used in the analysis is rendered unreliable, and, therefore, the conclusions are flawed. Once the machine spots any relevant event in the sales conversations we studied, it tagged when and where it occurred in the dialogue. We also factored in combinations or "sequences" of variables and added in several real-valued variables as well (e.g., sales rep talk time, silence time, interruptions, and overtalk).[1] Each of these could then be studied as an independent variable in our model.

For each call in our study, we were also provided with the "outcome" variable by the participating company—namely, did the sale ultimately close or not—as well as data about the seller's level of performance relative to his or her peers in the organization. For companies selling complex solutions, the "sale" will involve multiple calls across an often lengthy sales process, so we collected data across a time range that was long enough to allow for a sales cycle to be completed—and then added buffers on either end to ensure we were casting as broad a net as possible.

Putting this all together, we ended up with a massive regression model where we could say—with tremendous accuracy—what exactly happened in the sales conversation to drive the outcome we were studying. In total, the model calculated partial correlations for more than 8,300 independent variables with a dependent variable of a "closed sale." The final model proved to accurately predict outcomes more than 85 percent of the time. Once built, we tested the model against our larger data set of roughly 2.5 million sales calls.

The Gravitational Pull of the Status Quo

As our pipeline story illustrates, it can feel to sellers that losing to the status quo and losing to indecision are one and the same. After all, they result in an identical outcome—the customer failing to take action—and can therefore be hard for salespeople to tell apart. But our research and several decades of social science tell us, in no uncertain terms, that they could not be any more different. And assuming that they are one and the same is an extremely costly mistake for a salesperson.

Status quo bias is, simply put, a person's desire for things to remain as they are. Decades of research in the fields of cognitive psychology and behavioral economics—and the experiences of sellers in every market and industry the world over—teach us that this bias has a tremendous hold on us as human beings. In fact, researchers have found that people will opt for the status quo even when presented with options that entail low switching costs and would clearly make them better off. In the late 1980s, for example, economists William Samuelson and Richard Zeckhauser ran a series of experiments involving employees at Harvard University selecting their health benefits plans. They found that even when presented with a far superior plan with a better deductible and premium, more tenured employees tended to stick with the plans they had already chosen (compared to new employees who disproportionately chose the better plan from the menu of options).[2]

This happens for a few reasons, but the primary one is that change requires effort, and the unfortunate news—especially for salespeople whose job it is to *sell* change—is that people are genetically engineered to be lazy. Decades of research in the fields of biomedical physiology and kinesiology have demonstrated that the "principal of energy conservation" is hardwired into all animals, including humans. We are wired to choose the path of least resistance in any activity, choosing to minimize energy expenditure whenever possible. One fascinating study by physiologist Jessica Selinger and her colleagues showed that when fitted with a special leg brace that made normal walking more difficult, participants' nervous systems reflexively adjusted their gait to minimize caloric burn and exertion—without the participants themselves even being aware that it was happening.[3] So, finding the path of least resistance is something we do without even thinking about it. It takes a lot to get us to change.

The pull of the status quo becomes even more pronounced when we feel like we've passed up on better options in the past. Once somebody has a track record of passing up on better options, it makes it even less likely that they will act on an objectively good option that is sitting right in front of them—something behavioral economists call "inaction inertia." Realtors see this all the time. When buyers pass up or miss out on their dream home, it colors their perception of every other home they look at even if, in absolute terms, any of these other options represent a better situation than the buyer's current housing.

Salespeople are very familiar with status quo bias and encounter it all the time with customers. In our study, we found countless examples of customers falling back on the status quo as a reason not to move forward. Specifically, we found three flavors of status quo bias. The first type is when the customer expresses an actual preference for how they do things already. "This solution is interesting," said one customer, "although, I have to be honest, we've been pretty happy with our current provider." Another pointed out how much they'd already invested in building their current homegrown solution: "We've poured a ton of resources into building our own tool in-house. Granted, yours has a fair amount of capability that ours doesn't, but the powers that be won't like the idea of junking what we built."

The second type of status quo preference we found is when the customer doesn't agree that the supplier's solution represents a compelling enough alternative. One customer stated bluntly, "I'm not seeing much difference between your offering and the software we use now." Others were more diplomatic but just as clear that they weren't buying what the rep was selling: "I really appreciate the time you've spent with our team and I find what you guys are doing to be really interesting. It's going to take a lot for us to switch providers, but we should keep the dialogue going. The product road map vision you painted is very exciting."

Finally, some customers will agree that their "A state" is suboptimal and that the "B state" the vendor is pitching is much more compelling but will still revert back to their status quo because of their concern about the change involved. One customer said, "If you could wave a magic wand and get us from our current platform to yours instantly, this would be a slam dunk." Another expressed concerns that their department was short-staffed and it would be challenging to take on a project like what the vendor was proposing before they were back to full strength. And for another customer, the "baggage" of an earlier project that ended up taking twice as long as they were told by the vendor colored his perception of taking on similar initiatives, something he readily admitted was unfair, but still a reason his company was going to stand pat with their status quo: "In our experience, these things always end up taking at least twice as long as we're told. It's probably our own fault that this happens and I know it's not fair to hold it against you, but there's some skepticism around here when it comes to these sorts of implementations."

But the customer's preference for the status quo—as troublesome as it can be for sales reps to contend with—is still not the primary reason that deals end up lost to inaction. The bigger reason, we now know from our research, is that the customer is unable or unwilling to make a decision. In our study, we found that more than half of opportunities in which the customer states their intent to move away from their status quo nevertheless end up lost to inaction. But why would a customer who is *sold* on leaving their status quo behind *still* become indecisive and hesitate to take action?

The reason has to do with a psychological effect called the omission bias.

Nobody Likes to Lose

The omission bias derives from a concept psychologists refer to as "loss aversion," also known as prospect theory. In a series of now famous experiments, two Israeli psychologists and economists, Daniel Kahneman and Amos Tversky, demonstrated that people value the ability to minimize loss more than the ability to maximize gain.

For instance, when Kahneman and Tversky presented respondents with an opportunity to make a bet, they found that people tended to value the ability to increase their odds of winning from 90 percent to 100 percent *more* than they valued similar opportunities to improve their odds of winning from, say, 0 percent to

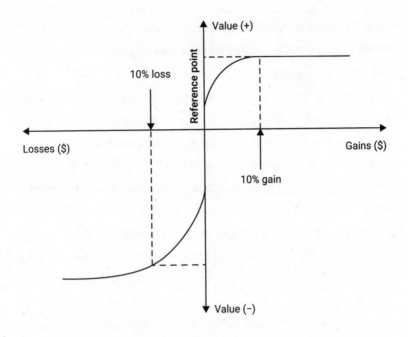

FIGURE 1.2: A graphical representation of prospect theory[4]

10 percent or from 50 percent to 60 percent (see Figure 1.2).[5] This finding flew in the face of conventional economic theory, which held that people would value each of these incremental improvements equally because they each represent a 10 percent improvement. But, Kahneman and Tversky found that these improvement opportunities are not equal in an individual's mind. Improving the odds of winning from 90 percent to 100 percent turned out to be valued more highly by respondents because of what it represents—an opportunity to eliminate the possibility of loss entirely—which isn't true for any of the other 10 percent improvement opportunities being offered. Rather than valuing these opportunities on their ability to maximize gain, people value them instead based on their relative ability to minimize loss. The duo found in their research that customers are actually *two to*

three times more likely to make a decision that enables them to avoid loss than they are to make a decision that enables them to realize a gain.

A simple illustration of how this works is to think about how you would feel if you found a one-hundred-dollar bill and then to compare that to how you would feel if you were to lose a one-hundred-dollar bill. Rationally speaking, you should feel exactly the same level of emotion whether you find or lose a one-hundred-dollar bill. After all, in either scenario, it's still the same dollar impact to you. But most of us don't feel this way at all. Instead, the negative emotions we feel when losing one hundred dollars are far stronger than the positive emotions we feel when we find the same amount of money. In layperson's terms, Kahneman explains, "People hate losing much more than they like winning."[6]

But, there is an important twist to their findings—one most salespeople, even those well-practiced in appealing to the customer's desire to avoid loss, fail to appreciate: all types of loss are not created equal.

Errors of Commission vs. Errors of Omission

In their research, Kahneman and Tversky found that we place more weight on loss that is the result of doing something wrong (what are known as "errors of commission") than we do on loss that is a result of failing to do something right (known as "errors of omission"). This phenomenon is called the omission bias. Simply put, this bias holds that people actually feel more regret when bad things result from their *actions* as opposed to when bad things happen as a result of their *inactions*.[7]

To illustrate, imagine a customer is weighing a significant purchase decision, like a new software platform that could change the course of her business. The new software seems to represent a way to avoid the significant maintenance costs and productivity drag associated with the current system the company uses. Now, let's say the customer chooses *not* to make the purchase and this results in an unrealized opportunity to improve her company's performance by ten million dollars. Now, consider the opposite. What if, instead of deciding *not* to make the investment, the customer decides to pull the trigger and sign the contract and, rather than proving to be a boon to her business, the whole thing backfires? Instead of closing productivity gaps and generating company growth, the investment leads to a ten-million-dollar *loss*. If you were in this customer's shoes, you'd probably rather sign up for the first ten-million-dollar loss than the second even though, objectively speaking, the loss is exactly the same in either situation.

So, yes, it's true that all customers want to avoid loss. But what they really want to avoid is loss that is the direct result of an action they took. Customers fear more the bad things that happen when they do *something* as opposed to the bad things that happen when they do *nothing*. They are, ultimately, more comfortable with *missing out* than they are with *messing up*.

Why We Feel So Strongly about Not Making Mistakes

Why do customers place more weight on loss that results from their actions than from their inactions? Part of the explanation lies in the fact that errors of commission are concrete. An error of commission is tangible and directly observable. Choosing to do one thing means you've decided not to do other things. You've effectively closed off other doors and possible courses of action from consideration. Errors of omission, on the other hand, are abstract and more difficult for the customer to measure and observe. Not deciding to make a specific decision could result in a loss . . . but you won't know for some time and, in certain cases, you may never know whether those losses ever materialize. The error of omission is a can the customer can kick down the road. The error of commission, on the other hand, is realized soon after the DocuSign is sent back to the vendor.

Another explanation is that errors of commission are personal in a way that errors of omission are not. Errors of commission are attributable to a person—even in a complex B2B purchase, there's always one person who chairs the buying committee, one person who makes the final decision, and one person who signs the agreement. An error of omission, on the other hand, could be anybody's fault. Opportunities come and go and it's hard to point to the person who committed the error or to the moment in which the error was committed. Everybody is culpable when it comes to sticking with the status quo, but *somebody* is personally responsible for changing it.

Consider the earlier example of the executive considering a new software platform for her business. If the customer makes the purchase and it goes sideways, it ultimately comes back to the person who signed the agreement and committed the budget and resources for the investment. But, what about choosing not to make the purchase and losing out on an opportunity to generate greater productivity and growth? Well, there were many other opportunities in the past to upgrade the system that the customer's predecessors chose not to pursue. And there were other members of the buying committee who expressed skepticism about the investment. There's plenty of blame to go around when choosing to do nothing.

Interestingly, researchers have found that over time, errors of omission start to feature more prominently in our minds than errors of commission—that is, once time has passed, the costs of having forgone previous opportunities is no longer abstract but instead becomes concrete to us.[8] In the same way, a customer might look back on a decision they didn't make several years before, and that lost opportunity may figure more prominently in their minds than decisions they actually did make. It's similar to when people are asked what their greatest regrets are in life: they will invariably point to opportunities they didn't take (e.g., the job they passed on, the concert they didn't go to, the house they didn't buy, the person they didn't ask on a date in college).[9] But, this does the salesperson little good. A purchase decision is something that needs to happen in the here and now. Sellers can't wait years for customers to reflect and only then realize they made a mistake. They need the customer to make a decision in the near term, whether that's by the end of the year, the quarter, the month, or by the end of a phone call.

This finding—that a customer's preference for the status quo and their desire to avoid making a mistake are, in fact, two different things—has been documented by researchers outside of sales as well. Psychologists Ilana Ritov and Jonathan Baron, for example, published a study in the early 1990s in which they sought to peel these two psychological effects apart.

"The term 'status quo bias' has been used to describe people's tendency of 'doing nothing or maintaining one's current or previous decision,'" they write. "Clearly, there are two claims embedded in this statement: the claim that people prefer to keep their current state of affairs, and the claim that people are reluctant to take action that will change this state."[10] In their study, participants were presented with different scenarios in which change will occur *unless* the participant takes action. They found that "subjects reacted more strongly to adverse outcomes caused by action, whether the status quo was maintained or not, and subjects preferred inaction over action even when inaction was associated with change."[11] Not only did Ritov and Baron find that status quo bias and omission bias—while they result in the same outcome, inaction—are two different psychological effects, but, of the two, it is the preference to avoid making a mistake that has the more powerful grip on us as human beings.

The omission bias helps explain why a customer who states their intent to abandon the status quo may still end up in a state of indecision, worrying over whether to take action. But it doesn't, in and of itself, explain what errors customers are so fearful of committing. Thankfully, the social science tells us what those are.

The Three Purchasing "Errors of Commission"

In 2003, researchers Veerle Germeijs and Paul de Boeck asked 174 graduating high school seniors to make decisions about college courses.[12] Respondents completed two questionnaires designed to determine where their indecision, if any, stemmed from. When they regressed the data, something fascinating emerged. It turns out that their indecision could be traced back to three specific fears.

First, some participants struggled with "valuation problems."

That is to say, they did not know how to value different options relative to one another and feared making the wrong choice from among a host of courses that seemed equally attractive. Second, some students became indecisive because of "lack of information." That is, they feared they hadn't done enough homework to make an informed choice. And, finally, some feared that they would fail to see the expected benefits from their decision. Germeijs and De Boeck refer to this as "outcome uncertainty." Even if they felt like they had enough information and were confident in picking one course over another, they nevertheless feared that they wouldn't actually realize the full benefits of their decision (e.g., Would the course actually help them prepare for their chosen professions?).

Our own study of sales conversations confirmed this finding. When we bucketed customers into the type of indecision they were experiencing, we found an identical pattern to what Germeijs and De Boeck found many years before—that there are, effectively, three reasons a customer might experience indecision: (1) they are worried about choosing the wrong option, (2) they are concerned that they haven't done enough homework, or (3) they fear they won't get what they're paying for (see Figure 1.3). Each of these, we found, has an associated set of behaviors and unique phrases and utterances—quite literally, things customers will say in a sales conversation—that serve as markers of their indecision.

In our study, the first fear—*valuation problems*—reared its head in a few different ways. Sometimes it came up when comparing feature sets across competitors. In one sales conversation, the customer said to the salesperson, "I know your system is cheaper to operate but your competitor's is much faster. We're trying to figure out what's most important to us as a business." Other

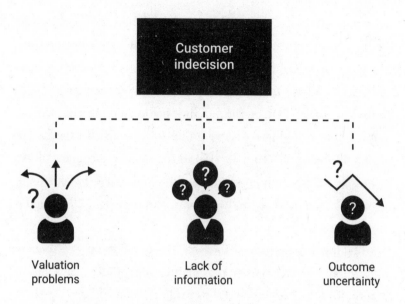

FIGURE 1.3: The three drivers of indecision

times, it showed up at the end of the sales process when the customer starts hemming and hawing over what the final contract should cover. Several customers wondered out loud what the best package was for their needs: "We're trying to figure out if we need to include the professional services component or if our team can do the work themselves," said one. Another ruminated about contract length: "I know we said we wanted to go with the three-year contract to lock in the price, but I'm now wondering if we shouldn't go back to the two-year agreement just to give us some more flexibility."

The second fear, *lack of information*, presented itself in sales conversations as the customer saying they needed to do more research before making a decision, despite having already consumed significant amounts of a seller's time, as well as that of their organization. They ask their reps to send more and more information to support their decision-making process. They ask them to have additional calls to address new questions that have come up since the last call. They enlist the help of third-party purchasing consultants to advise them on the purchase. And they invite more colleagues to weigh in on the purchase before making a decision— hoping that bringing a diverse group together with expertise in different areas will help them fill in the blanks. On one call, we heard the salesperson let out an audible sigh when his customer asked for "one more demo to just confirm that we are leaving no stone unturned."

The last fear—*outcome uncertainty*—is all about the "believability gap" between what reps claim their product or solution can do for the customer and the customer's confidence that these promised outcomes will, in fact, come true. Customers struggling with outcome uncertainty asked for endless references and seemed like they were basing their decision on reviews from other customers. Or they pressed reps on modeling out the exact returns they should expect—sometimes insisting on low-cost (or no-cost) proof-of-concept trials and pilots to validate that the solution worked and that it would generate the anticipated benefits or returns. "We're not going to pay for you to prove your product works," said one customer when the salesperson suggested the pilot the customer was asking for would entail a fee. "If this thing doesn't work for us, it's on me." They may believe the seller that their solution is valuable and unique, but they are still trying to figure out if it's going to deliver on what they need. It could be that the promised returns seem too good to be true. Or it could simply be that they lack experience using products like the one they're considering. Or perhaps their indecision stems from having been burned in the past by other vendors whose promises never materialized. Whatever the reason, these customers become incapacitated by the fear that they will make a mistake and be left holding the bag when the expected returns don't come to pass.

A Problem That Is Only Getting Worse

These drivers of indecision—valuation problems, lack of information, and outcome uncertainty—are not only problematic for salespeople *today*; they are likely to become a much bigger problem in the future.

With so many options being offered by vendors—and with an explosion of start-up players in almost every industry—customers find themselves unable to choose the right option. How does one company's unique feature or benefit compare to a completely different feature or benefit offered by a competitor? Similarly, the amount of information available to customers to evaluate products and services—not just from the companies that produce them but from expert analysts, reviewers, and everyday users— seems to grow exponentially every day, adding to the customer's concern that they haven't done enough homework to make an informed choice. And finally, as vendors push to increase the "stickiness" of their solutions—and therefore the cost, resource intensity, and risk associated with buying and implementing them— customers will increasingly find themselves wringing their hands over the question of whether all of the time, energy, and resources they're putting into a purchase will ever pay off or whether they'll be left having to answer for a bad decision.

In this sense, indecision is on a different trajectory than the status quo and is likely to only get worse with time. A customer's preference for the status quo is fairly monolithic and unchanging—it is the same today as it will be in the future. We'll always need to contend with the customer's aversion to change and desire for things to remain as they are. But indecision is driven by environmental factors that are beyond our control. It is not unreasonable to assume, then, that in the near future, indecision will account for an even greater share of losses due to inaction than it does today.

The "Silent Killer" of Sales

A big part of the challenge for salespeople—and one of the main reasons indecision has gone unrecognized for so long—is that it is difficult for a salesperson to detect in a conversation. Unlike the status quo, which customers will frequently discuss openly—stating that they prefer what they do today or that they don't believe the vendor's solution represents a more compelling alternative—indecision is rarely discussed in such terms. Because it's rooted in personal fears, it's something customers either don't feel comfortable admitting to or, more likely, are unaware is even affecting them and preventing them from making progress.

But, by leveraging natural language processing and machine learning, we are able to pick up on the emotions that are markers of indecision—emotions like uncertainty, confusion, anxiety, skepticism, and concern. Using this "carbon monoxide detector," we find that indecision is *everywhere*. A staggering 87 percent of all conversations in our study showed either moderate or high levels of customer indecision (see Figure 1.4). For a salesperson, finding a decisive customer is more like finding a needle in a haystack of indecision. While disqualifying deeply indecisive customers is a part of our story, which we'll discuss later on in the

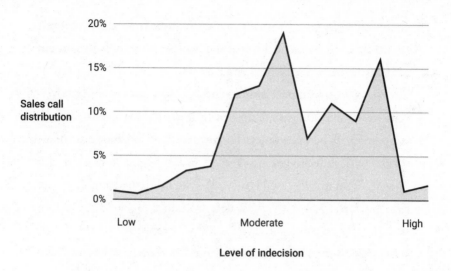

FIGURE 1.4: Sales call distribution by level of customer indecision

book, indecision is impossible to avoid in sales. In many respects, it's surprising that *more* deals don't end up lost to indecision.

When we separate out those calls in which customers verbalize their intention to buy, conversion rates—which one would have assumed would be sky-high—are actually far lower than expected, averaging around 26 percent. Instead of closing, a massive number of these sales fall apart for the seller, like a slow-motion train wreck. Despite expressing their intent to purchase early on in the sales process, these customers nevertheless start to voice significant levels of uncertainty and confusion. Emotions like these are, statistically speaking, some of the most damaging events in terms of impact on sales potential. And, when paired with objections—which occur on nearly 70 percent of the sales calls in our study—it is a toxic combination and, more often than not, a recipe for inaction. On call after call, prospects talked about shifting priorities and offered familiar refrains about past purchases they regretted making, ultimately pushing deals that felt as if they were at the goal line much farther away or taking them off the playing field altogether.

The corrosive impact of indecision on win rates is hard to overstate and something that most sales leaders don't even realize is happening. When customers start expressing the emotions we associate with indecisiveness, sales conversion begins to crater and it does so dramatically (see Figure 1.5). The more these emotions are expressed, the worse it gets. Where we found low levels of indecision in sales conversations, we found win rates in the 45–55 percent range. Just a moderate level of indecision drags win rates down into the 25–30 percent range. And where we see high levels of indecision, we found win rates below 5 percent. It's a success rate no better than throwing a dart at a dartboard—while blindfolded.

In the end, deals that seemed a sure thing ended not in a signature but in the customer saying they needed to "think about it."

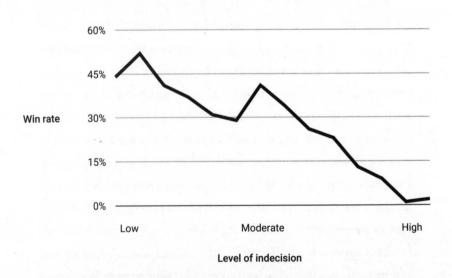

FIGURE 1.5: Impact of customer indecision on sales win rates

In fact, when we looked at our sample of sales calls and isolated only those opportunities where a customer had already expressed their intention to buy but nevertheless walked away without doing so, we found many phrases that were predictive of a lost sale. But, that one in particular—"I need to think about it some more"— proved to be more highly correlated with lost deals than any other across the tens of thousands of utterances we isolated in these calls. This phrase, statistically speaking, is the kiss of death. It is, in fact, actually *far worse* than being told no. It is the hallmark of customer indecision. One sales leader we interviewed called this the "warm hands, cold feet" phenomenon: when the customer *says* you've won their business but you still end up losing to "no decision."

But as troubling as all of this is, what is more troubling is that salespeople are unknowingly contributing to the problem.

Our Own Worst Enemy

In our study, we found that there was a remarkable consistency with which sellers tended to engage customers at the first sign they were getting cold feet. The default playbook—for the over-whelming majority of reps—is to assume the customer's status quo had not yet been defeated and, therefore, go back and try to defeat it again. We found this behavior on an astounding 73 percent of all sales calls in our study. What these reps actually sell may vary from company to company and industry to industry, but how they attempt to overcome customer indecision is remark-ably consistent.

This approach manifests in two different ways. Many reps attempt to reconvince the customer that their current state—the way they do things today—is suboptimal, if not unacceptable.

These sellers seek to "dial up the FUD" (i.e., fear, uncertainty, and doubt) in an apparent attempt to scare the customer into action. Alternatively, some reps try to resell the customer on the value of the future state—how great things could be if the customer moves forward with the purchase. These reps focus on re-proving the ROI of the purchase, reinforcing the vendor's value proposition and differentiation, or reeducating the customer on the features and benefits of the product they were once certain they wanted but are now starting to waver on. Regardless of which path is taken, these are two sides of the same coin: re-proving to the customer that they will succeed by making the purchase.

The problem, as seen through the eyes of the average salesperson, is that, despite the fact that the buyer is telling me they see value in our solution, they must not be fully convinced. They *say* they want our product or service, but there must still be an open question about *why* they should buy. If they really did believe in the *why*, then surely that would be enough motivation to push forward to action. So, if they hesitate, the average salesperson believes that, for whatever reason, they've not yet managed to break away from the gravitational pull of the customer's status quo.

And yet, despite the widespread use of an approach that's been handed down from leader to manager to salesperson for decades, our data shows—in equally stark and unrelenting terms—that it doesn't work. In fact, it backfires dramatically.

We found that when sellers attempt to "relitigate" the status quo with customers who've already expressed purchase intent, it generates a negative impact on sales outcomes 84 percent of the time (see Figure 1.6).

This possibility had never crossed our minds. The notion that

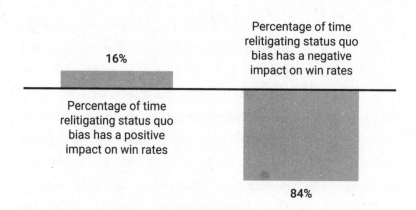

FIGURE 1.6: Impact of relitigating the status quo with indecisive customers

a hesitant customer is a customer who doesn't yet believe they will succeed by making the purchase seems so patently obvious that we never thought to question it. It's a concept that is woven into the conventional wisdom in sales. It's a topic that's been the subject of countless sales books. It's been the singular focus of nearly every sales training program and sales methodology in existence.

And yet, as widely accepted and used as this approach is, our data shows that it doesn't work to overcome customer indecision.

Why?

The reason is that, by definition, overcoming the status quo is about showing the customer how they will succeed by making the purchase and, by definition, what they stand to lose by doing nothing. It's about demonstrating the cost of inaction—showing what will happen if the status quo is maintained. By appealing to the customer's fear of missing out, we can get them to move forward, the thinking goes.

But as we've already discussed, customers are less concerned about loss that stems from their inactions than they are about loss that stems from their actions. Of course, the customer is already convinced of the cost of doing nothing—this is why they agreed to the vision you painted. But once they have agreed that they should move on from the status quo, the thing they now fear—and fear more—is the failure that may result from their actions: what will happen not if they do *nothing* but rather if they do *something*. And those costs will be both concrete and directly attributable to their decision.

This is why—for a customer who has agreed on a vision—it does no good for the salesperson to go back to the well, dial up the "pain of same," and convince the customer of what they stand to lose by maintaining the status quo because, at this point in the sale, that's not what the customer is worried about. Once they've stated their intent to move away from their status quo, the customer is no longer motivated by any of the abstract things that the seller is trying to draw the customer's attention to as they try to reconvince them. They aren't worried about missing a discount window or having to wait longer for a product to be back in stock. They aren't thinking about the fact that their team will have to wait another quarter before they replace the legacy system. They aren't concerned with losing ground to competitors. They aren't sweating the ongoing cost of maintaining the status quo. And they aren't fretting the upside opportunity or ROI they won't be capitalizing on.

Instead, the *only* thing they are concerned about is that they may be making a big mistake by purchasing your solution. All of the other concerns sellers try to leverage to motivate action pale in comparison to this. After all, you don't get fired for losing out on a 10 percent discount or having to wait another month for an implementation window. But you do get fired for spending money on a solution that fails to deliver the benefits it's supposed to deliver.

So, while it is good practice to build *intent* by showing the customer that the pain of same is worse than the pain of change, once the status quo is defeated and purchase intent is established, the calculus flips. To get from intent to *action*, the seller must now overcome the omission bias. Defeating the status quo may be all about showing the customer *how they will succeed with your solution*, but overcoming indecision is all about proving to the customer *that they won't fail by purchasing your solution.* When the customer becomes indecisive, it is typically *not* because they prefer the status quo. Instead, it's because they don't want to make an irreversible mistake. And while those two things sound identical, we now know that they couldn't be more different.

Readers likely now see how relitigating the status quo can be a waste of time when dealing with an indecisive customer who is already sold on the need to move away from the status quo. But you'll recall that we found this behavior not just to be unproductive, but actually *counterproductive.* Statistically speaking, the seller is better off doing *nothing* than trying to again convince the customer to change their status quo.

Why is this? How does relitigating the status quo actually hurt the seller?

To understand why, we need to think about the emotions sellers are looking to tap into when reconvincing the customer to abandon their status quo. When selling to the customer initially—before the customer offers their intent to purchase—reps will often lean more heavily on the "B state," painting a rosy and exciting picture for the customer. And when the customer starts to waver and show frustrating signs of indecision, sellers tend to then paint a dark picture for the customer, dialing up the fear, uncertainty, and doubt that they hope will scare the customer into action.

Fundamentally, this approach is about tapping into the customer's fears—fear that they'll be stuck with a suboptimal status quo or fear that they'll miss out on a golden opportunity to capture benefits or upside previously unattainable. But, as we've already discussed, *fear* is ultimately what is causing the customer to *be* indecisive. Namely, that they are about to make a big mistake. And so, piling more fear on top of the customer's existing fears tends to backfire dramatically for the salesperson, as it just gives the customer more to be worried about, *more* reason to feel stuck, and *more* justification for kicking the can down the road. Simply put, trying to scare an already scared customer into buying is a terrible sales strategy.

Conclusion

In this chapter, we've learned that the bigger driver of losses due to inaction is not preference for the status quo; it's customer indecision, which is driven by the omission bias (i.e., the customer's desire to avoid making a mistake).

The omission bias is powerful and, ultimately, a far bigger obstacle for the salesperson to overcome than convincing the customer that their status quo is suboptimal. Not only that, but the fears that drive indecision—valuation problems, lack of information, and outcome uncertainty—are fed by environmental factors beyond any of our control. As options offered by vendors become more numerous, information available to buyers continues to pile up, and the cost and risk of solutions increases, the likelihood a customer will become stuck and mired in their own indecision goes up as well. And, finally, when it comes to indecision, salespeople are often their own worst enemies—not only have they never been taught how to detect it, but by continuing to relitigate the status quo with customers who are, in fact, struggling with indecision, they increase the customer's level of fear, anxiety, and indecision, making it more likely their deal will end up stalling out and ultimately be lost to inaction.

The customer's desire to avoid losses that are the direct result of their actions is, unfortunately, something that average performers misdiagnose all the time. Ultimately, average performers struggle to convert sales that are sitting right at the finish line because they deploy a playbook designed for beating the status quo, not one purpose-built for overcoming indecision. When a customer is already sold on the new way forward, that life will be better with your company's product or service, no amount of reconvincing them of these things will overcome what's standing in the way of them signing on the dotted line. Getting them across the finish line requires a fundamentally different approach. Our research shows that the best sellers have figured out that there is a point in the sale where their job is no longer convincing the customer how they'll *succeed* by making the purchase; it's about proving to the customer that they won't *fail* by making the purchase.

In the next chapter, we'll share the surprising playbook high performers deploy for overcoming customer indecision as revealed through our analysis of more than 2.5 million sales conversations.

CHAPTER TWO

The JOLT Effect

S o far, we've established a few things.

First, indecision is a big problem for salespeople. Our research shows that it has a toxic effect on win rates *and* that it happens all the time—in all types of sales, across both transactional and complex sales. It is a problem that robs sellers of productivity and effectiveness and one that represents a massive opportunity cost for sales organizations and companies. And it's a problem that shows no signs of letting up. If anything, it's likely to get worse. As suppliers flood the market with content, introducing new offerings and options, and as fast-moving, disruptive start-ups pop up in nearly every industry, the reasons for customers to hit the pause button and take more time to mull over a purchase decision are only becoming more numerous.

Second, the well-worn playbook most sellers use to overcome indecision fails to do so—in fact, it fails dramatically. At the end of the day, sellers have only ever been equipped to do one thing:

beat the status quo. And the techniques they've been taught for doing so—most notably appealing to the "pain of same"—backfires when applied to the task of overcoming customer indecision and actually getting customers to act on their intentions.

What's clear is that salespeople today need to be equipped with two playbooks, not just one. Where average performers believe that the sale is simply about beating the status quo and appealing to the customer's desire to avoid the "pain of same," the best sellers know that there is a second phase—between agreement on a vision and an actual purchase decision—where things can, and often do, go off the rails. This second phase is about dealing with the fears that are preventing the customer from being able to move forward. This—in and of itself—is a highly surprising finding in light of the decades of management attention and sales training investment that has been devoted to only the first part of the sale. There is a surprising dearth of research, books, and training content on the second phase of the sale, and yet, without successfully traversing from intent to action, sellers still face an incredibly high probability of finding their deal stuck in the land of indecision.

Make no mistake, defeating the status quo will always be a key component of any sale. If a seller cannot break the gravitational pull of the status quo, she has no hopes of selling anything. But as the status quo is defeated and starts to recede, it is replaced by a second, more menacing foe: the customer's own indecision, which is driven by a set of errors they are desperate to avoid committing. If the playbook for beating the status quo is predicated on dialing *up* the fear of *not* purchasing, the playbook for overcoming customer indecision is about dialing *down* the fear *of* purchasing.

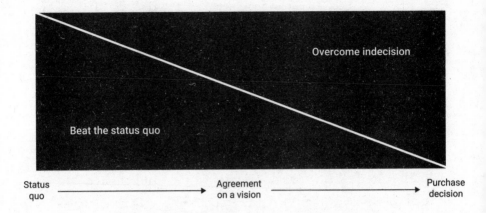

FIGURE 2.1: The two playbooks for sales effectiveness

The best way for salespeople to think of these two playbooks is that they work in tandem across the sales process (see Figure 2.1). When a salesperson first engages a customer in their status quo— and across the early stages of the sale—the most important thing for a rep to do is to defeat the status quo. Once the customer's intent is secured and the status quo fades into the background, what comes to fill the vacuum and take its place is the customer's own indecision. The fear of missing out is replaced by the fear of messing up. If the salesperson has any hopes of bridging the gap between intent and action, she must at this point subordinate the playbook for beating the status quo to the playbook for overcoming indecision.

Importantly, overcoming indecision is not merely an approach for closing—that is, overcoming late-stage customer hesitancy and solving the "last mile" problems that sellers are so familiar with. Best reps know that while indecision is unlikely to fully rear its head until the salesperson puts the status quo to bed and gets the customer to agree on a vision, it's important for the salesperson to be attuned to signs of customer indecision that may start appearing in the very first interaction. These star sellers know that indecision can creep in at any point in the sales process and that to avoid the problem of customers taking "one step forward, two steps back," the seller must be constantly vigilant—from the first moment of the sale to the last.

So, what's in this second playbook? How exactly do high performers overcome customer indecision?

The JOLT Method

Our research reveals that high performers execute a unique playbook when dealing with stuck customers—one purpose-built for overcoming indecision that is, in many respects, the opposite not only of what they've been taught to do over the years but also the opposite of the approach they take to beat the status quo. We call this playbook the JOLT method.

The first behavior we identified in our research was "judging the indecision." In a series of interviews we conducted with high-performing salespeople, we found that they qualify and disqualify opportunities in a different way from average salespeople. While it's long been known that high performers qualify opportunities based on *externally* observable criteria (e.g., use case fit, industry attractiveness, company dynamics), our research reveals that they also qualify opportunities based on less observable but nonetheless critical criteria based on the customer's own ability to make decisions. Put another way, they qualify not just on *ability to buy* but also on *ability to decide.*

The purpose of this is twofold. First, it enables them to disqualify hopelessly stuck customers. In our study, we found that high performers were disproportionately more likely to disqualify opportunities in which the customer seemed intractably indecisive. Through a combination of indecision-focused diagnosis, active listening, and careful observation, they are able to ascertain whether the customer *can be* motivated to take action or whether it is a lost cause. Unlike their average-performing peers for whom "hope springs eternal," top sellers seem to have an innate sense for the likelihood that a customer can be guided out of their indecision and whether it's worth their time and energy to do so. And, second, when they determine that a customer is not hopelessly stuck but may still be struggling with some level of indecision, it enables them to understand the degree to which they need to lean into their indecision playbook or, at the very least, how to forecast the deal.

The next behavior in the JOLT method is "offer your recommendation." When working with customers struggling with valuation problems—concerned about picking from among what seem like equally attractive options—we found that the approach most salespeople take is to rely on needs diagnosis. These reps defer to the customer and use a bevy of questions to try to surface what's really important to the customer. But high performers know that customers who are indecisive are looking for guidance, not more choice. And so, they take a decidedly different approach. Rather than *asking* confused customers what they want, they instead *tell* them what they should buy (e.g., "These are all good options, but personally, here's what I would do if I were you"). In doing so, they make a decision that can feel overwhelming and complicated for the customer instead feel streamlined and achievable, ultimately increasing the odds that the customer will move forward, not back.

The third behavior we uncovered was "limiting the exploration." The overwhelming amount of information available to customers to research and evaluate opportunities and providers is the bane of every salesperson's existence because it feeds the customer's perception that they haven't done enough homework to make an informed purchase decision—the "lack of information" problem we discussed in chapter 1. But where average performers see themselves as purveyors of information for customers—indulging every request they have for more information, be that an additional white paper, another demo, or one more reference call—high performers seem to know that no amount of additional information will ever satisfy the customer's desire for more and that it is ultimately impossible for customers to consume all of the information out there to inform a purchase decision. So rather than continuing to feed the customer's request for more, high performers limit the exploration by controlling the flow of information, anticipating needs and addressing unstated objections, and practicing radical candor when customers dig in and insist on superfluous amounts of information. To earn the right to do this, they know that they must establish themselves as subject matter experts who are both credible (i.e., they know more than the customer about the decision the customer is trying to make) and trustworthy (i.e., they help the customer see that their guidance is rooted not in what will enable them to sell more but instead in what is in the customer's best interests).

The fourth and final behavior in the JOLT method is "take risk off the table." When faced with customers who start to fret about outcome uncertainty—whether they will get the benefits they hope for—our data shows that average performers tend to counter this concern by directing the customers' attention away from what they might lose by making the purchase and back toward what they stand to lose by *not* making the purchase. In other words, they take a classic FUD approach to try to scare the customer into making a decision. High performers, however, understand that there is a time and a place where showing customers the cost of inaction can be useful—namely, when trying to overcome the status quo and gain agreement on a vision. But, once this is accomplished, continuing to dial up the "pain of same" is counterproductive since customers become more concerned about potential loss related to their actions, not inactions. And chief among these concerns is the customer's deep fear that they will be left high and dry, held accountable for purchases that end up not delivering their intended benefits.

To overcome the customer's outcome uncertainty, high performers focus not on scaring the customer into buying but on coming up with creative solutions that limit downside risk (e.g., opt-outs, refund and change clauses, additional professional services support, contract carve-outs). At the same time, they seek to manage customer expectations as to when and to what degree returns will be realized and to put in place guardrails that make the customer feel like losing is a very low-probability outcome (e.g., "I've mapped out our first three months together to show you exactly what we're going to do to get some quick wins"). Finally, in contrast to much of the conventional wisdom out there that high-quality sales are always bigger and more expansive, we found that high performers can overcome outcome uncertainty by recommending to customers that they instead start small, generate early wins, and then expand from there. Ironically, they ultimately sell more by selling less up front.

Together, these four techniques comprise the JOLT method—*judge* the indecision, *offer* your recommendation, *limit* the exploration, and *take* risk off the table. It's the playbook high performers use to get their customers *unstuck*, overcoming their indecision and, ultimately, *jolting* them into action. As we explore each of these techniques in more detail, we'll share both the compelling empirical evidence that these techniques work as well as the evidence from social science that helps explain *why* these techniques are so effective.

The JOLT Effect

Before we dive into each of these behaviors, we need to understand what the payoff is. Any sales leader who has ever tried to roll out a new methodology or sales approach can attest to the fact that driving change at the front line is hard—it takes time, commitment, and investment. So the return has to be worth it in order to consider pushing yet another new set of behaviors onto their salespeople.

Here, there is good news for sales leaders. In no uncertain terms, our analysis reveals not only that these behaviors are worth considering but that leaders would be hard-pressed to find *any* investment that can deliver the win rate improvements that we see with this new playbook.

Because these techniques are not commonly taught in the typical sales training class—and, in some cases, are the opposite of what's being taught—we don't see them very often in real sales calls. Of the calls we studied, fully one-third showed either a low or a completely undetectable level of JOLT skill demonstration. And only 7 percent of all calls showed a high level of JOLT skill demonstration. Suffice it to say, there is room for improvement for the vast majority of salespeople.

But the data also clearly shows that learning how to apply

the techniques that comprise the JOLT method can be a clear difference-maker for salespeople when dealing with customer indecision. Recall from chapter 1 that relitigating the status quo—when used alone as a technique for overcoming customer indecision—has a *negative* impact on win rates 84 percent of the time. But what happens when sellers instead use a JOLT approach? What happens, then, when sellers don't just rely on *inducing* fear but instead use JOLT for *reducing* it? When this happens, sellers go from an 84 percent probability of a bad outcome to a 70 percent probability of a good one.

When we break out the data, we see JOLT sellers delivering higher win rates across all levels of customer indecision than what the average seller is able to produce (see Figure 2.2).

First, consider customers experiencing low levels of indecision. Decisive customers make everybody look like they're good at sales. And, not surprisingly, both average performers and JOLT sellers convert well above the average win rate of 26 percent. In these rare situations, average sellers convert at 39 percent while top performers land nearly 70 percent of their opportunities. But,

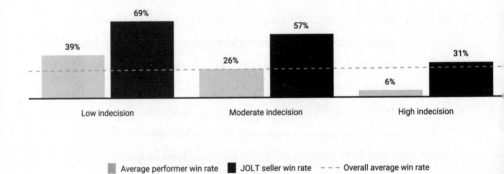

FIGURE 2.2: Average seller vs. JOLT seller win
rates by level of customer indecision

as we discussed previously, decisive customers are hard to come by. Instead, the vast majority of opportunities—87 percent, to be exact—are with customers experiencing either moderate or high levels of indecision. And as soon as customer indecision spikes, average performers regress back to the mean, converting at 26 percent, while their JOLT seller counterparts still maintain a conversion rate of 57 percent. That is nearly a 120 percent difference. In fact, this is the greatest delta between core reps and stars that we see in the data. Finally, when we look at the highly indecisive customers, average rep win rates fall off a cliff. These reps win only 6 percent of these deals. Comparatively, even with these customers who are the *most* mired in indecision of any segment we see in the data, sellers using JOLT behaviors *still* manage to convert above the average, at 31 percent.

For a company handling hundreds (and in some cases, thousands) of sales interactions a year, even getting reps to move from "not very good" to "pretty good" represents a potentially huge improvement in revenue generation—just by focusing attention on this small set of key behaviors.

And there's one more benefit to this approach: Because these behaviors help instill confidence in the buyer that they are making a good decision and are successfully going to avoid the loss that they fear may befall them, they help avoid what psychologists call "post-decision dysfunction"—that is, the tendency of people to regret their decisions, revisit them, and, in some cases, reverse their decisions after they've been made. In this way, the JOLT method isn't simply an approach for boosting win rates; it's an approach that boosts loyalty and mitigates post-sale customer churn. This is something we'll revisit in more detail in chapter 8.

Conclusion

In this chapter, we introduced the high-performer playbook for overcoming indecision. Our research shows that high performers do four things that separate them from their peers: (1) they *judge the indecision*, diagnosing sources of indecision and ascertaining their likelihood of overcoming them; (2) they simplify the decision by *offering their recommendation* as opposed to endlessly asking the customer what they want to buy; (3) they *limit the exploration* by shutting off unproductive lines of inquiry, discouraging customers from spinning their wheels doing additional research; and (4) they *take risk off the table* by managing expectations and offering creative "safety net" options that give the customer confidence they won't be left in the lurch. These techniques together represent a new playbook for *jolting* customers out of their indecision.

Across the next four chapters, we will explore each of these high-performer techniques in more detail—sharing not just the evidence as to why they work but guidance for how to apply them in sales conversations.

CHAPTER THREE

Judge the Indecision

In our research, customer indecision was a constant, appearing at the same level in wins as in losses. It's not something a salesperson can make "go away" as much as it is something to deal with and navigate through. And yet, a curious finding emerged as we started looking at pipeline makeup through an indecision lens: high performers actually had far *fewer* opportunities in which customers displayed high levels of indecision and far *more* decisive customers in their pipelines.

One high-performing medical device salesperson we interviewed helped us to decipher what we'd stumbled upon. "There are two things I'm always looking for with any customer," she said, "their ability to *buy* and their ability to *decide*. Most of my colleagues are pretty good about qualifying opportunities based on standard fit criteria, but they end up spinning their wheels on customers that look good on paper but will never pull the trigger."

For her, indecision is as much something to be identified and understood early on in the sale—in order to determine *how* or even *whether* to pursue an opportunity—as much as it is something to be managed later.

She went on to share two stories to illustrate how, in her mind, screening an opportunity for indecision can help her spot deals that are dead before they even start as well as promising opportunities that other salespeople might overlook. One was a hospital that should have been a perfect fit for her company's solution. "They were a big hospital and they were growing fast. Not only that, but they weren't happy with their current equipment and were looking for a new solution that would grow with them as their needs evolved. We were really the only option for them. But it became pretty clear to me right away that even though we were in a 'category of one,' the customer couldn't get out of their own way. They asked for an endless number of references, a long pilot—that they refused to pay for—and all sorts of guarantees that were going to be impossible for me to give them. So, while it was a big potential opportunity, I kicked it to the back burner and told my manager I was spending my time elsewhere and that I would engage with them when they were ready, but I wasn't forecasting them to come in anytime soon."

The other story was a medical center that was really small by her company's standards—barely large enough to hit their radar screen—and they still had several years of life left on their existing lab equipment. "But," the rep explained, "while this wasn't a great prospect on paper, the lab director was extremely decisive. From the get-go, he trusted me to guide him to the right solution and actually turned down offers I made to set up reference calls—which is pretty standard in our business—saying that he knew we had a great reputation and didn't think it was a great spend of his time or our customers' time for them to tell him something he already knows. I could tell right away that this one was going to be a fast close for me. And, despite the ribbing I got from my team for spending time on the opportunity, it was the fastest deal we closed all year."

Judging Customer Indecision

Any salesperson will tell you that getting a customer to actually make a decision is often easier said than done. The journey between the verbal commitment and the signed agreement, between selection and transaction, between "I want to" and "I did" can be a slog. But how long will the journey take? How deep is the customer's indecision and, therefore, how much effort will it take for the salesperson to bridge the gap between agreement on a vision and a purchase decision? What, specifically, is the cause of the customer's indecision? If the customer is so deeply mired in indecision, is it even worth the salesperson's time and effort to try to get them over the line?

Figuring all of this out is absolutely critical. This is why "judging the indecision" is the first and, arguably, most important step in the JOLT method.

For the rest of this chapter, we'll discuss how salespeople can identify the source and depth of the customer's indecision, as well as how to take into account potentially exacerbating factors that can make a customer's indecision worse.

Pinpointing the Source of Indecision

As we discussed in chapter 1, there are three sources of customer indecision: valuation problems, lack of information, and outcome uncertainty. The first step is understanding which of these are driving the customer's indecision.

In our study, we found that each of the three sources of indecision copresented with specific phrases and utterances from customers. Summing these up surfaces a set of indicators as to the source of the customer's indecision. First, let's consider valuation problems. Again, this is when the customer is stuck between options and expresses confusion or uncertainty about which one is best for their needs. When it comes to valuation problems, reps should ask themselves:

- Does the customer quickly point to options and configurations that they prefer or do they seem to want it all (e.g., "This all looks compelling to me")?
- Does the customer continue to press on differences between various packages and configurations (e.g., "Can you explain again the difference between . . . ?")?
- Does the customer ever openly express confusion about which option to go with (e.g., "We're stuck between this option and that one")?
- Does the customer get distracted by new discoveries such as features and options they didn't know about before (e.g., "We didn't realize you had this capability. Can you tell us more?")?

Next, we have lack of information. This is when the customer feels anxiety or confusion over their perception that they haven't done enough research or homework to make an informed purchase decision. Here, reps should ask themselves:

- Does the customer ask for more of any sort of input (demos, reference calls, conversations with solutions engineers or subject matter experts, etc.) than the typical customer?
- Does the customer ever delay in the name of collecting more information?
- Does the customer ever say they're feeling overwhelmed by all of the information out there?
- Does the customer express concern about "being in the dark" or "still far up the learning curve"?

The third and final source of indecision is outcome uncertainty. This is when customers express concern, skepticism, or anxiety about the returns they'll see from their purchase and if, in the end, they'll get what they're paying for. Here, reps should ask themselves:

- Does the customer press you for ROI projections (and revisions of those projections)?
- Does the customer reference other investments that they've been burned on in the past?
- Does the customer talk about how big a risk or investment your solution is relative to other things they've done in the past?
- Does the customer ask for guarantees or assurance of results?
- Does the customer express skepticism about outcome achievability?

Answering these questions can help reps narrow in on the source of the customer's anxiety, which will help the salesperson to know which of the "plays" they'll need to run to overcome the customer's indecision—whether offering their recommendation, limiting the exploration, or taking risk off the table—all of which we'll discuss in more detail throughout the rest of this book.

But so far, we've only ascertained the source of the customer's indecision, not the depth of it. We may know what's driving the customer's indecision, but not how difficult it will ultimately be to close the deal. To understand that, we need to factor in two additional dimensions: the customer's personal level of indecisiveness and external factors that can exacerbate indecision.

Gauging a Customer's Personal Level of Indecisiveness

Sometimes, it's easy to tell when someone is struggling with indecision. Consider the friend who asks the waiter to come back multiple times and then asks everybody else to put their order in first . . . only to then ask the waiter to help him decide between two equally appealing options. Or, maybe you know somebody who puts their holiday shopping off until the last minute? One fascinating study by DePaul University professor Joseph Ferrari in the early 1990s aimed to understand the reasons that some people put off holiday shopping until very late. In this experiment, researchers interviewed Christmas shoppers in a local mall at four different intervals: four weeks, three weeks, and one week before Christmas as well as the weekend immediately before the holiday. They found that it was indecision about what gifts to buy—not dislike of shopping or other competing commitments—that caused shoppers to delay.[1]

But, at the end of the day, because indecision is a "state of mind" more than anything, it can feel like something that would be hard to detect in a sales conversation. After all, how can we tell the difference between the customer who is mired in indecision and the customer who is just going through a measured and deliberate purchasing process, which we all know can take time depending on the product or service the customer is considering? How do we know when the customer is just moving slowly or is, in fact, well and truly *stuck*? Fortunately, the social science has some answers for us.

Since at least the 1970s, psychologists and behavioral economists have been trying to answer a whole host of questions around why people fail to make decisions, even when the outcomes of those decisions would seem to make them better off. Through thousands of experiments and data-based studies, they have sought to understand how people perceive the decisions before them, what influences the way in which they perceive those decisions, how indecision manifests in terms of real-life behaviors, and whether there are conditions under which people tend to become more or less indecisive.

Because indecision is so hard to pin down—even (and perhaps especially) for the person suffering from it—psychologists developed an instrument known as the "Indecisiveness Scale," which enables them to assess a person's level of indecision. This tool, developed in 1993 by Randy Frost and Deanna Shows, has become the gold standard for assessing indecision.[2] The instrument itself comprises fifteen statements that respondents are asked to rate themselves against:

- I try to put off making decisions.
- I always know exactly what I want.
- I find it easy to make decisions.
- I have a hard time planning my free time.
- I like to be in a position to make decisions.
- Once I make a decision, I feel fairly confident that it is a good one.
- When ordering from a menu, I usually find it difficult to decide what to get.
- I usually make decisions quickly.
- Once I make a decision, I stop worrying about it.
- I become anxious when making a decision.
- I often worry about making the wrong decision.
- After I have chosen or decided something, I often believe I've made the wrong choice or decision.
- I do not get assignments done on time because I cannot decide what to do first.
- I have trouble completing assignments because I can't prioritize what is most important.
- It seems that deciding on the most trivial thing takes me a long time.

In multiple follow-on studies, the scale has proven to be highly correlated with the behaviors we tend to associate with indecision. For example, in one experiment, Frost and Shows asked fifteen respondents who scored low on the Indecisiveness Scale and fifteen who scored high to make a series of fifty decisions. Participants had to choose twenty college courses out of forty offered, twenty pieces of clothing to keep out of a pile of forty, and, finally, a favorite meal from three different restaurant menus. In the end, the indecisive participants took nearly fourteen minutes to complete the required tasks compared to less than nine minutes for the decisive participants.[3]

But short of asking every customer to fill out the Indecisiveness Scale questionnaire before we start selling to them (!), what can salespeople do to assess the customer's level of indecision?

To figure this out, we dug into our mountain of sales call data to surface potential "tells" that customers give—signals they send—that cause high performers to pump the brakes. We then went back to test these findings with star salespeople through a series of interviews, and what came out was a simple four-step process that can be used by any salesperson to assess a customer's indecisiveness and decision-making dysfunction—that is, the things that negatively impact the customer's "ability to decide."

Step one is understanding how the customer searches for and consumes information. While we know that "lack of information" is a source of indecision that all customers encounter, some customers have a higher comfort level with ambiguity than others, which is something a salesperson needs to detect early on. Second, we need to look at how the customer evaluates alternatives. Is their evaluation process logical and structured or is it frenetic and hard to pin down? Third, we need to look for signs that tell us whether the customer is willing to settle for "good enough" or whether they won't be satisfied unless everything about our product perfectly suits their needs. Finally, when the customer starts to hesitate, backpedal, and waver, salespeople need to be able to "read the tea leaves" and interpret the indecision signals that different types of delay provide.

For the remainder of this chapter, we'll discuss each of these steps, explaining the social science behind it as well as the "tells" high performers look for to gauge the customer's indecisiveness. Knowing the answers to these questions can be the difference between a deal that is appropriately prioritized, resourced, and forecast and one that ends up pushing out into eternity, withering on the vine, and dying a slow death.

How Does the Customer Search For and Consume Information?

Every salesperson knows that while they have their own sales process, a customer has their corresponding buying process and that it's critical to understand how one maps to the other (see Figure 3.1). But great salespeople seem to understand that there are a few key points where the customer's own indecisiveness will reveal itself. One of these is how the customer searches for and consumes information.

Today, it's common for customers to do a fair amount of research on their own before ever reaching out to a supplier. In our research at CEB (now, Gartner), we found that the average customer is nearly 60 percent of the way through the buying jour-

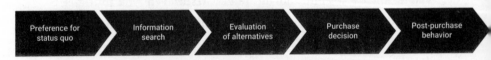

| Preference for status quo | Information search | Evaluation of alternatives | Purchase decision | Post-purchase behavior |

FIGURE 3.1: Representative customer buying process

ney before they ever make contact with a supplier.[4] And when the customer finally does make contact with a salesperson, their learning accelerates dramatically. We set up demos, run pilots, and have customers engage with our subject matter experts, solutions engineers, product team members, and customer success managers.

To be clear, it's perfectly normal for customers to seek out and consume information to inform their purchases, and as much as salespeople would prefer that the customer just take their word for it and not consume a lot of information, this is unlikely to happen—especially with more expensive, disruptive, and complex products (and even more so when we're talking about new, untested technologies). It's rare today that a customer *won't* take the time to do research, read reviews, call reference customers, and fully investigate a supplier's offerings. So, doing research doesn't, in and of itself, mean that a customer is indecisive. Instead, what high performers look for is the *amount* of information the customer requires to feel confident and the *way* in which they seek that information.

High performers know, intuitively, that there is a big difference between normal amounts of research or due diligence and when the amount of information requested tips over into the zone of "analysis paralysis"—or research for research's sake. When this happens, these reps know they're dealing with a customer who is inherently uncomfortable with ambiguity. For those customers who have a low tolerance for ambiguity, researchers have found, it doesn't just create hesitancy in making decisions but conjures up negative emotions like worry and regret—a recipe for disaster for any salesperson.[5]

The second "tell" high performers look for when determining

if a customer is comfortable with ambiguity is what behavior psychologists call "backtracking." This is when customers seem to be making progress through their buying process but then, suddenly, new information presents itself and the customer starts to move in reverse. One high performer we interviewed told us that a big red flag for her is when a customer is engaged in a later-stage activity like a pilot or negotiation on a proposal and suddenly learns of some new piece of information like an analyst report or a start-up player they hadn't heard of up to that point. She told the story of a customer who she'd been engaged with for three months. Her company had just completed a successful pilot with the customer and had entered into contract negotiations with procurement and legal when the customer dropped a bombshell: "I hate to do this," the customer said, "but, as you know, the new Gartner Magic Quadrant just came out and, I'm embarrassed to admit this, but there are a couple of providers that they have highlighted as up-and-comers in the space but we've never heard of, let alone talked to. We just want to check the box and talk to them before we make our final decision. We still want to move forward on the contracting front with your company—we're pretty sure these other guys really aren't at the same level as your company—but, as you know, this is a big decision for us and we want to make sure we're leaving no stone unturned. Hopefully you appreciate the seriousness with which we're taking this decision." The rep told us that she knew, then and there, that the customer would never make a decision and the deal wasn't going to close. "I politely told the customer that we want to completely respect their process and would put contract negotiations on hold until they decided that they wanted to move forward with us. That was six months ago. And they still haven't made a decision on how to move forward."

How Does the Customer Evaluate Alternatives?

Another step in the customer's buying process that can present telling signals of indecisiveness is the way in which customers evaluate alternatives. High performers we interviewed tell us that, in this stage, they are paying attention to whether the customer, when comparing different providers and options, is able to do so in a logical and structured way or if they're haphazardly comparing apples and oranges.

Psychologists Joseph Ferrari and John Dovidio explain that "indecision is more than not making timely decisions."[6] At its core, indecision is a form of decision-making dysfunction and we can spot this dysfunction by looking not just at what happens *before* the decision, but by looking at the *way* a customer makes a decision. Numerous studies, for example, have found that indecision tends to copresent with a tendency for a person to think "intradimensionally"—that is to say, focusing on one attribute as most important (e.g., price), researching it exhaustively, and then pulling up the tent stakes and switching to a different attribute (e.g., reliability) and starting all over. For salespeople, this presents as the customer who is laser-focused on a single feature or capability and ignores everything else (even those attributes that would provide the customer with more value), only to later change their minds and decide that this feature isn't actually the most important one to them after all. These customers may ultimately make a decision, but the way they get there is convoluted and hard to make sense of—which, of course, suggests a high probability that the customer will end up second-guessing their decision and potentially later reverse it.

A related decision-making dysfunction is the inability of some people to engage in efficient choice evaluation when faced with multiple options—something researcher Christopher Anderson has studied at length.[7] When facing such decisions, he argues, people engage in one of two different decision-making approaches. The first he calls "compensatory selection"—that is, the tendency to weigh and trade off different criteria against one another. For instance, when thinking about a new mobile phone, the slower processing speed or lower storage of one device might be compensated for by its lower price or the fact that it comes with additional accessories that other devices do not. Compensatory selection can cause customers to become indecisive because of the inherent difficulty in comparing criteria that are, in effect, apples and oranges. Decision makers using this strategy tend to produce more suboptimal choices, he explains.[8]

Some of the difficulty in weighing diverse criteria against one another can be reduced or eliminated by taking what he calls a "noncompensatory" selection approach. In this approach, certain criteria are considered in more of a binary way—either they're critical or they aren't, and if something is critical, any option that doesn't have it is eliminated. This is another reason that RFPs are used in purchasing, especially for expensive, complex solutions. With so many different features and benefits of different suppliers' offerings, companies will often use an RFP to narrow down vendors to a short list containing only those offerings that check the box on "must-have" criteria.

For instance, let's say a company is considering a new CRM system. There may be more than a dozen vendors in their consideration set, but an RFP can help get the list down to a more manageable group of three to four vendors that provide the capabilities a customer knows it can't live without (e.g., that the vendor have expertise and experience in their industry, that the cost per seat license not be above a certain level, or that the solution can be deployed by in-house staff without heavy reliance on a vendor's professional services team). Once the short list is created, a customer might then shift into more of a compensatory selection approach—in other words, they've determined that any of those providers who made the cut can do the job and now it's just a matter of picking which of the remaining competitors offers the best value.

This is even commonplace today in the consumer world. Consider Amazon as an example. Given their significant inventory—which can lead to customers getting lost among many seemingly equal, attractive options—they have structured the buying journey to make it easy for a customer to "chalk the field" around what's most important, compare options, and make a decision. Consider, as an example, a customer looking to purchase a new television. Shoppers can quickly prioritize what's most important by using filters like average customer rating, screen size, features, manufacturers, and price range. Doing so quickly gets the customer from hundreds of products down to a handful that fit the bill. And, when a customer clicks on one of the options on their short list, Amazon shows a small table comparing the selected option against a narrow set of other choices customers also considered. In this way, Amazon subtly encourages a noncompensatory selection approach to narrow down a vast number of options to get the customer to a smaller consideration set quickly. Years of collecting customer behavior data has shown them that when customers spin their wheels looking through a sea of choices, they are far less likely to buy something than if they are looking at a smaller set of curated options.

The real question for a high-performing salesperson is whether a customer who is *not* engaged in a formal purchasing process like an RFP can independently structure their evaluation process in a logical and explainable manner. "A warning sign for me," one star rep told us, "is when customers struggle to explain how they created their short list of vendors they're talking to. They typically won't tell me who else they're talking to, but they should be able to tell me what the 'must have' criteria were that they used to filter down to a smaller number of providers—as well as which criteria were deemed less important. If they can't explain their criteria, that tells me they're not going about this in a way that's going to lead to a decision."

Reps, of course, have their ways of figuring out who else is competing for the customer's business and this rep was no different. But what was different was that this rep used this knowledge as an indicator of the customer's indecisiveness: "There are certain competitors I always expect customers to talk to. They do good work and it's in the same vein as what we do. There's nothing wrong with them being on the short list with us. Now, we may *say* that comparing us to these other players is comparing apples and oranges . . . but at least the customer's comparing different types of *fruit*. But when I learn through the grapevine that the customer has included providers whose solutions aren't even in the same zip code as ours, that's a really bad sign. Comparing apples to oranges is one thing but comparing apples to Tuesday is something else altogether. Those customers I deprioritize because, at the end of the day, they don't know what they want."

Is the Customer Content with "Good Enough"?

Every salesperson knows that sales is not a "game of perfect." They know that their company's products and services, while better than their competitors' in key respects, probably fall short on others. They know that not every customer or analyst is going to give their solution top marks across the board. And even the best product demo, pilot, or proof of concept will have hiccups and speed bumps. The real question is whether your customer is okay with this.

In 1956, economist and Nobel Prize winner Herbert Simon introduced the idea that there are fundamentally two types of people when it comes to making decisions: "satisficers" and "maximizers."[9] Satisficers are fine with "good enough" when making choices and decisions. Once they find the option that satisfies their requirements, they choose it—even if there might be better options out there. But, for a maximizer, there is no such thing as good enough. Instead, "good" is more of an absolute concept. This isn't to say they don't have criteria that are more or less important to them—they do. But when they find an option that meets those criteria, their inclination is not to pick it but to keep looking for that option that might *better* fit their criteria. "Consider, for example, the choice of college," psychologist Shahram Heshmat explains. "In order to determine their optimal decision outcome, maximizers feel compelled to examine each and every alternative available. Maximizers rely heavily on external sources for evaluation. Rather than asking themselves if they enjoy their choice, they are more likely to evaluate their choice based on its reputation, social status, and other external cues. In contrast, a satisficer asks whether her college choice is excellent and meets her needs, not whether it is really 'the best.'"[10]

The research shows that maximizers actually make better decisions (i.e., they end up selecting the superior option)—but, despite this, they end up being less happy with their decisions. In a study of college graduates, Arne Roets and his colleagues found that maximizers chose jobs that paid 20 percent more than those that satisficers chose. But, interestingly, those maximizers in the study were less pleased with their job selections than their peers.[11] Ultimately, being a maximizer leads one to perpetually second-guess one's decisions and make comparisons with others whom one perceives to have made better decisions. Put simply, all of the extra research and diligence a maximizer puts in certainly pays off—but to what end if you're ultimately unhappy with your decision and wondering what could have been.

Most behavioral economists agree that there is no such thing as a "pure maximizer" simply because it's impossible for a person to consume and process all of the information about every option available before making a decision. Therefore, maximizing is in some way a practical impossibility—whether because of the limits of human cognition, limited time available to make a decision, or lack of perfect information available to evaluate options. This is why, for all intents and purposes, most people end up satisficing as a shortcut to making a decision. But still, we know that in the real world, this doesn't stop many customers from looking for perfection. Customers are often more than happy to "let the perfect be the enemy of the good."

High performers tell us that they are always on the lookout for those customers who want perfection and choose to focus on perceived shortcomings rather than the benefits they may see by making the purchase. One salesperson we interviewed told us that she always asks after any customer interaction—whether something small like a sales call with the buying committee or a demo, or something bigger like a trial or a proof-of-concept—for her main point of contact to tell her how it went. "I want to know where we hit the mark and where we missed. And when the customer replies, I'm always reading between the lines. Did they lead with the things that went badly or the things that went well? Do they list more things that went well or more things that didn't? How do they talk about the things that went poorly? For example, are they planting the seeds of failure or are they simply offering opportunities for improvement?"

She went on to illustrate with an example: "When we do a pilot, there are always some hiccups in terms of getting started just because we haven't integrated into the customer's existing systems yet. So things end up being fairly manual up front and I always forewarn my main point of contact about this. But not all customers react the same way when I ask at the end for feedback on how it went. I can have two pilots that go *exactly* the same way and one customer will say, 'Boy, getting the pilot going was a real bear for our team' or 'I'm going to need to do some damage control here' while another customer will respond by saying 'It took a little more work to get things up and running but you told us to expect that and once we were rolling, the platform performed exactly as we hoped.' Just based on that feedback, I can tell whether the opportunity is going to move quickly or whether it's going to be a knock-down, drag-out battle to get it across the line."

What Is the Nature of the Customer's Delay Tactics?

Even high performers can miss signs of customer indecision until they actually manifest in purchasing delays. Of all the behaviors associated with indecisiveness, delay—that is, when we fail to make a decision in a timely fashion—is the behavior we most commonly associate with it.[12] Salespeople can attest to this fact since they would roundly agree that *all* customers delay. But, as we learned from the social science and from our high-performer interviews, not all delays are created equal.

Decades of social science research reveal that there are, in fact, two inherently different *types* of delay: procrastination and decision avoidance.

Procrastination is something many of us can relate to—the act of putting something off until the very last moment or past its deadline. This behavior is actually quite common. Joseph Ferrari explains that "everyone procrastinates, but not everyone is a procrastinator. We all put tasks off, but . . . research has found that 20 percent of US men and women are chronic procrastinators. They delay at home, work, school and in relationships. These 20 percent make procrastination their way of life, so of course they procrastinate when filing their income taxes. We are a nation of 'doers' but we are also, like people from other industrialized nations, a people of 'waiters.'"[13] A separate study actually found that 80–95 percent of college students procrastinate (which any reader with college-age kids will probably find less surprising

than the fact that 20 percent of the entire US population are procrastinators).[14]

For salespeople, it sometimes seems like every customer is a
procrastinator. It's quite common for deals today to result in heel-
dragging by customers. It's not that they aren't making progress
toward a decision, it's just that they seem to come up with every
excuse in the book for not making one today. These delays take
many forms—sometimes they're a function of protracted back-
and-forth with corporate departments like legal or long delays in
getting required information to a salesperson. These delays can
feel inexplicable because, in many respects, they are. Customers
don't give you a "no," but more of a "not yet" . . . and it can seem
like any effort to push them faster is met with either indifference
or outright resistance.

Psychologist Eric Rassin argues that there are several reasons
people procrastinate: "Some people are reluctant to start activities
because they are insecure about their capacity to complete them.
For these individuals, procrastination is a way to temporarily deal
with possible disappointment and blows to self-esteem. Others
shift activities because they like or 'need' deadline pressure to perform at their best . . . [But] while procrastination has several
attributed causes, indecision is likely to be one of them."[15]

Procrastination, however, differs from the other, more nefarious reason that customers delay making decisions: decision avoidance. When a customer procrastinates, they still *intend* to act even
though they are temporarily putting it off. Decision avoidance
has no such intention. "Decision avoidance," Christopher Anderson explains, "manifests itself as a tendency to avoid making a
choice by postponing it or seeking an easy way out that involves
no action or no change."[16] Put another way, a procrastinator delays

making a decision for many reasons, but a decision avoider delays for only one reason: *so as not to have to make a decision.*

Decision avoidance is also, unfortunately, not uncommon, and psychologists like Anderson have argued that the tendency to avoid decisions is becoming more common, especially in Western society where people are bombarded with endless choices and information about various options—something we'll discuss in the next two chapters.[17] What's more, decision avoidance is inextricably linked to human beings' natural desire to avoid unnecessary effort. As Rassin argues, "Generally, living creatures strive to reach goals as cheaply as possible. Thus, if one does not have to decide, it seems only logical to not make a decision."[18]

For a seller, decision avoidance is like the evil twin of procrastination. And, because they can often manifest in similar ways, salespeople can confuse a delay with merely being a sign that the customer is procrastinating when, in fact, it's really that the customer has no intention of making a decision at all. Obviously, salespeople need to not only be aware of the difference between procrastination and decision avoidance but to look for "tells" that can help them determine which of these is driving the delay. Misdiagnosing a delay as procrastination when it's something far worse can lead to an overly optimistic assessment by the salesperson. These are the opportunities in which frustrated sales managers often find themselves having to step in and kill for cause—but not before countless days, weeks, and months have already been spent trying to coax the deal across the line . . . time that could have (and should have) been spent on opportunities more likely to close.

How do sellers spot the difference between a customer who is procrastinating and a customer who is avoiding making a decision altogether? High performers told us that they can spot the difference simply in the *way* the customer delays. To quote one rep we interviewed, "It's one thing for a customer to cancel a call scheduled for this week and ask if we can push [it] out to next week . . . but it's another thing entirely when the customer tells me 'now's not the right time' or 'priorities are shifting' and then asks if we can pick up the dialogue next month, next quarter or next year. Those customers have no intention of ever making a decision and either they haven't figured that out themselves or they just don't want to rain on my parade so they keep it to themselves. Either way, when I hear that, I stop spending time with them and usually kick myself because I should have figured that out sooner."

When customers don't send up clear red flags like these, we found that high performers tend to rely on "powerful requests" to elicit a response from the customer that will allow them to understand what's driving the delay they are experiencing.[19] For instance, these sellers would request that a hesitant customer arrange a meeting with key buying group members or with corporate leaders in IT, legal, HR, finance, or procurement to gauge whether they are dragging their heels or whether there is something else holding up progress. If a customer doesn't intend to make a decision, requests like these—particularly when the customer is being asked to consume the time of busy colleagues—can be revealing. If the customer agrees to get colleagues involved in the decision-making process, it can provide verification of positive intent and forward momentum. If not, it can signal a more deep-seated reluctance to move the deal forward and, ultimately, to make a purchase decision.

Sometimes, figuring out what's driving the delay is as simple as asking. One telling example came to us from the CEO of a tech company who told us that he ran into a customer who one of his salespeople had been pursuing for months while at a conference. "These folks seemed like they were primed to buy," he told us, "and the salesperson on the deal forecasted it to close every week . . . which then turned into six months. So, when I spotted the customer at this event, I asked him if he would grab coffee with me and, when we sat down, I asked him if there was something going on that I should know about." The customer then explained that priorities were shifting at their organization, so the CEO asked what the new priorities were. When he listed them, the CEO replied, "As you know, our solution will directly impact four of the six priorities you guys have. So, I'm wondering if there's something else that has you concerned?" After some continued probing, he finally learned the real reason why they kept pushing the decision: the customer himself had lobbied for a significant investment in another platform the year before and, when he made the business case to the CFO, he said that this investment would solve a whole range of problems for the organization. But it turned out that this platform wasn't actually capable of all they thought it was. The salesperson had oversold them. "So, this is why they are now talking to us," the CEO explained. "But, more to the point, the customer said he now has egg on his face and he's dreading the meeting with the CFO to ask for a new slug of investment for our platform."

In the end, this CEO told us that surfacing the real reason behind the customer's continued delays did two things for his team. First, it enabled them to focus their time on helping the customer prepare for that conversation. And, perhaps more importantly, it told them that this deal shouldn't be forecasted to close anytime soon and should be deprioritized by the sales team. He said, "It was painful to reforecast a big deal that was sitting right at the goal line, but at the end of the day, it was more painful to continue allocating time and resources on a deal that is actually more of a long shot than a sure thing."

Exacerbating Factors

The psychological research on indecision also points to a number of external factors—whether based on time (e.g., "You have only until the end of the week to make this decision") or the perceived importance of the decision (i.e., the cost of the product or service being considered or the potential ramifications if a bad decision is made)—that can amplify a customer's indecisiveness, making it more likely a deal will be lost to inaction.

To test the effects of decision importance on indecisiveness, for instance, researcher Robert Ladouceur and his colleagues asked two groups of volunteers to sort different colored pills. The first group was simply asked to sort them by color but the second group was told that the pills were being shipped to a country where few people could read. For this second group, it was therefore critical that the different-colored pills be sorted correctly or people might suffer adverse medical reactions. The group that was given this additional "pressure factor" spent considerably more time hesitating and rechecking their work compared to the group that was simply asked to sort the pills by color.[20] For their part, salespeople know that as the magnitude of a decision creeps up— because of an escalating price tag or impact on a personal or business level—it can bring deals to a grinding halt. Decision importance can turn even seemingly decisive customers into indecisive handwringers.

Time pressure is another exacerbating factor that can increase the propensity of a customer to get stuck. Ironically, applying time pressure is a technique often used by sellers to get customers to sign on the dotted line—"exploding offers" and limited-time price guarantees or discounts are age-old tools for getting a customer to purchase today when they would, all things being equal, prefer to wait. This is something we'll explore in more detail across the rest of this book, but our data also clearly points to the ineffectiveness of such pressure-selling tactics. If anything, they make it more likely for the customer to be indecisive, not less.

Putting It All Together

When we consider the four dimensions of indecisiveness high performers look for—how the customer consumes information, how the customer makes trade-offs, whether the customer is content with "good enough," and the way in which the customer is delaying their decision—a compelling framework emerges, one that allows all sellers to spot and judge customer indecision like the best salespeople (see Figure 3.2).

For each dimension in this scorecard, a salesperson would rate a customer—the lower the score on any given dimension, the more decisive they are and the higher the score, the more indecisive. As a rule of thumb, opportunities that score more than twenty-two points total are candidates for disqualification—or, at the very least, are candidates for deprioritization by the salesperson and more careful scrutiny by sales managers (see **www.jolteffect.com** for

Comfort with ambiguity	1	2	3	4	5	6	7	Need for certainty
Structured alternative comparison	1	2	3	4	5	6	7	Unstructured alternative comparison
Satisficer	1	2	3	4	5	6	7	Maximizer
Procrastination	1	2	3	4	5	6	7	Decision avoidance

An opportunity scoring more than twenty-two points on the scorecard should be considered for disqualification

FIGURE 3.2: Scorecard for assessing a customer's level of indecision

an interactive version of this scorecard). When scoring a customer opportunity, sellers must also consider the exacerbating factors we've discussed—such as decision importance and time pressure. Even if a customer scores on the more decisive end of the spectrum, such mitigating circumstances can amplify latent tendencies and predispositions, rendering seemingly good opportunities on paper ones that should instead be deprioritized or even disqualified altogether.

Conclusion

Best salespeople know that their time is their scarcest resource. And while it's long been known that star reps qualify and disqualify opportunities aggressively, we've always assumed that this was done largely (if not exclusively) on "external" criteria like industry, company financials, available budget, existence of compatible legacy systems and processes, and so on. But what we hadn't fully appreciated until now is that high performers also disqualify opportunities based on "internal" criteria—namely, the degree of indecision displayed by a customer. While these sellers have the confidence to know that they *could* win a deal even with a deeply indecisive customer, they also have the wisdom to know when their time is better spent elsewhere. As the rep whose story we shared at the beginning of this chapter so aptly put it, salespeople need to gauge not just a customer's *ability to buy* but also their *ability to decide.*

We also learned about the four key screens that together form an indecision "acid test" for the high-performing seller to use in assessing the depth of a customer's indecision. Best salespeople will spot the difference between a customer who is comfortable with ambiguity and one who needs certainty before making a decision; a customer who is able to engage in a structured comparison of alternatives and one who is not; a customer who is content with "good enough" and one who isn't happy with anything less than perfection; and a customer who is procrastinating versus one who is avoiding the decision altogether.

They will also take into account exacerbating factors like importance of the decision and time pressure as conditions that might amplify otherwise modest levels of indecision and lead to a deal that may become irrevocably stuck. And, whether won or lost, best sellers ask the same question in the end: What can be learned from this opportunity that can better prepare me for the next one?

If there's one clear conclusion readers should draw from our discussion so far, it is this: feeling overwhelmed, immobilized, and otherwise unable to make a decision is a decidedly human phenomenon—a perfectly normal customer behavior. In many respects, it's hardwired into who we are as people. But knowing how to spot the signs of intractable indecision—and to make the hard decision about disqualifying or deprioritizing an opportunity that might look great on paper but is never ultimately going to close (or that *may* close but will likely exhibit post-decision dysfunction)—is one of the key skills of high-performing sellers.

In the next chapter, we'll explore the next high-performer behavior: offering your recommendation.

CHAPTER FOUR

Offer Your Recommendation

In his groundbreaking book *The Paradox of Choice: Why More Is Less*, psychologist Barry Schwartz shares a terrific story about his own experience shopping for a pair of jeans. Gone are the days when there was only one type of jeans on the shelf. Nowadays, you've got every cut, color, wash, and fabric imaginable: straight fit, bootcut, loose fit, tapered, blue, black, stonewashed, distressed, button fly, zip fly, you name it. Expecting to be in and out of the store quickly since he knew his jean size, Schwartz was instead presented with a multitude of options and, while he ended up selecting one, he didn't feel great about the choice and walked out of the store wondering if perhaps he should've gone with a different pair.

Schwartz goes on to depict the multitude of choices we face as consumers today—from salad dressings in the grocery store to the options wireless providers offer for mobile phones and data plans to the various configurations and support plans offered by B2B software providers. And it's not just the product world where this view has taken over. The desire to give customers more choice has permeated nearly every aspect of our lives. In health care today, he explains, doctors are far less likely to tell patients what they should do and far more likely to lay out various options for treatment, each with pros and cons. Even when pressed to offer an opinion, these physicians typically decline—instead suggesting that the choice is ultimately the patient's to make. Western industrial society, he argues, is built on this fundamental belief: "The more choice people have, the more freedom they will have and the more freedom they have, the greater their welfare." "This [belief]," he explains in his well-known TED Talk, "is so deeply embedded in the water supply that it wouldn't occur to anyone to question it."[1]

But the problem is that the endless array of options we face—while seemingly a good thing—actually has the opposite effect on us. When we face an abundance of choices, we end up not liberated but, in fact, frozen in place by our own indecision. Any of us who have faced a decision about what to buy—whether that's something consequential like a house, a piece of software to help run a business, or a decision about our own health care, or something as inconsequential as a mobile phone or a pair of shoes—can relate to Schwartz's story about buying something and then immediately second-guessing the choice we just made. In the end, customers who *want to buy* end up struggling with how to value the different alternatives sitting in front of them and, ultimately, doing nothing.

Why does this happen? Schwartz contends that choice makes

people miserable for a few specific reasons. First, as choice increases, so too does the potential for making a bad choice. And, because of the anticipated regret effect that we discussed earlier in the book, it leads to people sitting on the sidelines, making no choice whatsoever. This is a common phenomenon in any sales situation, whether consumer or business. Customers know they want the product or service they're being sold. The rep successfully overcomes the customer's status quo bias. But then the customer starts handwringing about *what exactly* to buy.

The consumer starts to wonder if they should just spring for the phone with more storage. It's a three-year contract and they don't want to run out of storage after a year or two . . . but, then again, the higher-capacity model is *a lot* more expensive, well beyond what they'd planned to spend on a phone. Similarly, the business customer stares at the DocuSign in their inbox, ready to commit to the purchase, but they hesitate: Do they really need the premium version of the software or will the standard version be sufficient for their company's needs? They could see their organization taking advantage of some of the advanced features and they certainly looked impressive in the demo . . . but the last thing they can afford is to spend scarce budget dollars on capabilities that end up going unused. In short, the more options we put in front of the customer, the more they tend to hit the pause button—or, in some cases, step away from the sale altogether. Better to do nothing, the customer rationalizes, than to make a bad purchase.

One vivid illustration of how customers, when presented with too many options, tend to sit on the fence comes from the retirement plan provider Vanguard. Research done on retirement accounts showed that for every ten investment funds an employer offered its employees, participation rates actually *fell* by 2 percent —meaning that for a company that offered fifty funds, its employees would participate at a 10 percent lower rate than that of a company that offered a small handful of choices (see Figure 4.1).[2]

Another reason that excessive choice tends to undermine decision-making progress, Schwartz explains, is that even *if* we are able to make a decision that is, objectively speaking, a good choice, we end up being less satisfied with it because we wonder whether we could have made a better choice. This sort of "post-decision dysfunction"—which we'll discuss more in chapter 8— is a hallmark of customer indecision. Oftentimes in sales, we are able—through sheer force of will—to get a hesitant customer

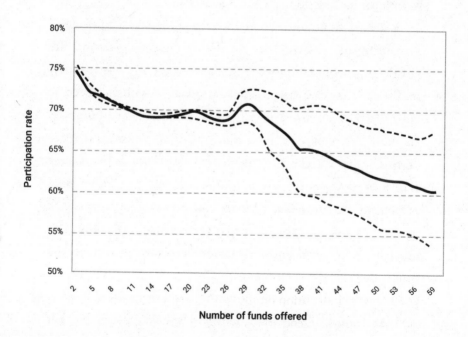

FIGURE 4.1: Employee participation rate in
401(k) plans vs. number of funds offered[3]

over the finish line. But what Schwartz and others have found is that *making a decision* is often not the end of a customer's indecision; it's just the beginning. For a customer, the nagging thoughts they have about "what could have been" will stand in the way of them fully embracing the purchase they've just made. This isn't just a recipe for unhappy customers; it's a first step toward a back-out and churn.

Third, Schwartz argues, as we face more options, the bar for what will satisfy us continues to escalate, ultimately making us feel like we are "settling" for any option we choose. Readers will remember the issue with satisficing and maximizing we discussed in the previous chapter. Satisficers are those individuals who are looking to max out *certain* attributes in a decision, whereas maximizers are looking to maximize *all* attributes.

A deeply troubling notion for sales leaders and salespeople to contemplate is that many of the customers we assume are satisficers—because of how easily they made trade-offs and how readily they express their intent to purchase—will later become maximizers when asked to actually consummate the purchase. It's much easier for customers to be satisficers when it comes to expressing intent. The customer saying they *want* to buy is easy and doesn't cost them anything or entail any risk (other than perhaps losing some face with the salesperson). So, it shouldn't be surprising to salespeople that customers make effortless, confident trade-offs early on. Everybody's decisive when it doesn't count. But actually *acting* entails a lot of risk. Things can always go wrong once the ink is on the contract and the product is delivered. And when they do, somebody will be held accountable. For this reason, the customer's latent maximizer tendencies become magnified late in the buying process. At signature time, customers who were once decisive get cold feet. They hem and haw and ask for every assurance that nothing will go wrong—that they won't be abandoned. Decisiveness goes out the window when it's time to sign on the dotted line.

Finally, Schwartz argues that choice makes us unhappy because we blame ourselves when we feel like we made the wrong choice. This is the error of commission problem readers will recall from earlier in the book. An error of commission is when we feel we've lost out because of something we did: for instance, if we personally chose the wrong product or we signed the agreement without negotiating for a lower price or we prioritized the wrong features and benefits when picking the solution for our business. This is different from an error of omission, which is when we lose out because of something we didn't do. An example of this might be missing out on the cryptocurrency run-up because we chose not to invest in cryptocurrency.

We started our discussion in this book by framing the customer indecision problem as one rooted in *loss aversion*—a concept we later explained has its roots in prospect theory. This is undeniably true: while the early stage of the sale might be largely about convincing the customer how to avoid loss that stems from their *inactions*, the back half of the sale is all about how to avoid loss that stems from their *actions*. And this fear of loss is much more acute when the customer looks around and realizes that *if* this purchase results in a loss or some avoidable negative outcome, they will *personally* be the one shouldering the blame.

Consider the customer who is about to change his family's homeowners insurance provider. What if something happens—a burst pipe, for example—and he realizes that while the old policy covered these situations, the new one does not? Who can he blame when explaining to his partner what happened? It was his fault for making the change in providers and not considering important coverage differences. Or, consider the manager who is spearheading a purchase committee evaluating a large investment for their company. At the end of the day, the committee plays a role, but that manager is ultimately the person who puts her badge on the desk and says to the higher-up, "I'm recommending we go with this vendor." And when things later go sideways, that manager will be the same person who will feel the consequences of having wasted the company's time, money, and resources on a purchase that didn't pan out. Loss is something all customers want to avoid. But loss that they are personally responsible for is something they want to avoid like the plague.

The Choice Dilemma

All of this evidence that choice overwhelms customers might make the solution feel obvious: pare down the choice set so that customers don't struggle with the valuation problems that can lead to indecision. But it turns out, it's not that simple.

While it seems like minimizing the choice set for customers would make it easier to get to a purchase decision, there is also ample data to suggest that customers are actually drawn to the *idea* of more options, especially early on in the buying journey. It's only later in the journey that these same choices become problematic. This is what researchers Sheena Iyengar and Mark Lepper found in their now famous "jelly" experiment. To test the effect the number of options had on customers, they set up a table at a local grocery store with twenty-four different flavors of jelly available for customers to sample and purchase. The abundant number of options proved to be enticing to those entering the store as 60 percent of visitors stopped by the table to sample one of the options. But while many shoppers sampled, only 3 percent ended up buying a jar. Then, on a different day, they set up their table again, but this time offered only six types of jelly to sample. The limited number of options was less appealing to visitors, as only 40 percent sampled one. But, the narrower set of choices led to a much higher conversion rate: 30 percent of those who came by the table ended up buying a jar.[4] The solution, then, isn't to eliminate choices altogether for customers; it's to know *when it's time* to shrink the consideration set in order to drive the customer toward a decision.

High performers seem to know this intuitively—that there is a time for letting a thousand flowers bloom and a time for telling the customer which one to pick. In our study of sales calls, we found that just like their average-performing colleagues, high performers will engage early on in diagnosis and using probing questions to understand the customer's wants and needs, but at some point, they purposefully eliminate options from consideration by *making a recommendation* to the customer about what they should buy.

Two Skills Needed for Effective Recommendations

In our study, two skills in particular jumped out as indicative of this sort of approach. The first we call "proactive guidance," which is when the rep shifts from a reactive posture (i.e., "Help

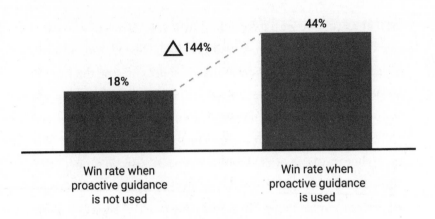

FIGURE 4.2: Impact of proactive guidance on win rates

me understand your needs") to a proactive posture (i.e., "Here's what you need"). Proactive guidance has a demonstrably positive effect on win rates. In our analysis, we found that win rates jump from 18 percent to 44 percent when reps used this one skill—an improvement of 144 percent (see Figure 4.2).

What does proactive guidance sound like in practice? In many respects, it sounds like a subtle nudge, a small bit of direction offered to a customer. "This configuration is our most popular," one rep explained. Another pointed out that "most of our new customers start with this plan and then upgrade later as their needs evolve." On occasion, we found this guidance being offered after the customer had indicated some hesitation about the decision they were being asked to make. These reps were likely seeking to avoid a situation in which they recommend one option and the customer has already decided they prefer a different option—therefore potentially making the customer feel foolish for preferring something else. As soon as high performers sensed indecision and uncertainty start to creep in, they immediately offered some guidance to help narrow the playing field of options and thereby move the customer closer to the finish line. But, as effective as this approach was, we found that high performers more frequently offered their recommendations *before* the customer expressed any confusion about how to value the different choices in front of them. This technique—anticipating needs and objections—is something we'll explore in more detail in the next chapter.

More powerful than making a general recommendation, however, was when the rep offered his or her *personal* recommendation. We call this behavior "advocacy" because it suggests not just that the rep is personally advocating for a specific choice but also because the salesperson is indicating that they are *on the customer's side* in making this decision. They feel personally responsible for the customer making a good choice and look to show the customer what they would do if it were their money and their decision to make.

We found these star reps saying to their customers, "Here's what I would do if I were you" and "I always tell customers they can't go wrong with X." These reps are able to do this because, as we'll discuss later in the book, they've already established that they are trustworthy experts—somebody who is not just in a position to offer guidance to the customer but also can be trusted not to make a biased recommendation in the interest of closing a bigger deal. The personal wrapper they apply to their recommendation takes what was a gentle nudge or piece of information (e.g., "This is a popular option") and puts their personal seal of approval on it (e.g., "I personally prefer this option")—something that amplifies the win rate lift that can be realized through guidance alone. In our study, we found that this advocacy technique by itself can lift win rates by 74 percent (see Figure 4.3).

When used in combination, proactive guidance and advocacy are a powerful one-two punch for overcoming valuation problems. These techniques are used by high performers to break the "paradox of choice" that Schwartz tells us can so often lead to purchase regret, post-decision dysfunction, and, often, no decision at all.

In our analysis, we broke out sales calls by how frequently reps used this combination of skills and what the associated impact was on win rate. We found that roughly 40 percent of the time, sellers used neither of these techniques and, as a result, saw conversion rates as low as 13 percent. When reps used at least one of

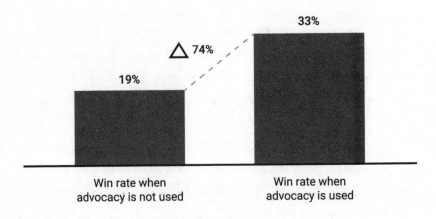

FIGURE 4.3: Impact of advocacy on win rates

these techniques, conversion rates jumped above the average in our study, to 29 percent. And in the rare 16 percent of calls in which we found both techniques being used, win rates were a whopping 48 percent (see Figure 4.4).

Not surprisingly, our analysis shows that when customers *aren't* deeply indecisive, these "recommend" techniques improve win rates substantially. When we look at instances in which customers are experiencing low levels of indecision, we see a 240 percent difference in win rates when recommend skills are demonstrated at a high level compared to a low level (see Figure 4.5). This is a huge increase, to be sure. But techniques like those we've discussed in this chapter produce a natural lift in any scenario, not just the "easy" ones. When we look at the conversion rate lift in the hardest calls (the ones with the greatest indecision), it is orders of magnitude greater—530 percent, to be exact. While the

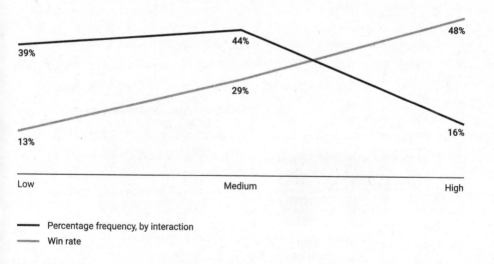

FIGURE 4.4: Frequency of "recommend" skill demonstration and impact on win rates

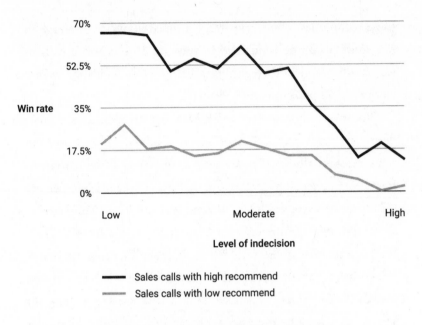

FIGURE 4.5: Win rate impact of recommend
skills by level of customer indecision

absolute win rates are always going to be lower in these situations, this delta is explained by the fact that, when confronted with high levels of indecision, average performers cave entirely. The win rates we see where there are high levels of customer indecision and low levels of rep skill demonstration are below 2 percent. High performers, by contrast, lean on their recommend skills and still salvage a 13 percent win rate.

How to Avoid Amplifying Indecision

As important as it is to use these skills to make powerful recommendations—recommendations that can overcome the customer's indecision about what to choose—it's equally, if not more, important to know what to avoid doing.

By and large, average performers meet the customer's indecision about what they should buy not with a recommendation but with more questions: "What's important to you?," "What are you looking for in a solution?," "Are there questions I can answer for you that would help you decide?" They respond in exactly the way they've been trained to respond: rather than leading the customer and guiding them to a decision, they defer to the customer and let their indecision run rampant. This tendency to be reactive and responsive to customer needs rather than being prescriptive has been so ingrained in salespeople for so long that it comes across as a knee-jerk reaction, something almost instinctual.

To be clear, diagnosing needs and asking probing questions isn't definitionally a *bad* thing. After all, we found that these sorts of questions can have a positive impact on win rates when used up front in the sales conversation (because they help the rep calibrate their approach based on what the customer has already done and what they've already learned before engaging the salesperson). But when used in the face of customer indecision—when the customer is clearly stumped about which of the many options facing them is the right one to choose—this approach can backfire, and significantly so. In our study, we found that when reps diagnose needs *and* offer their personal recommendation, win rates are 36 percent, well above the average of 26 percent in all calls. But, when reps engage in "open-ended diagnosis"—that is, diagnosing needs but not offering any sort of recommendation—win rates plummet to 14 percent (see Figure 4.6).

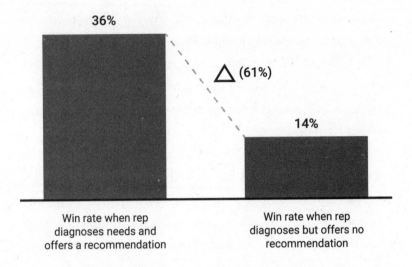

FIGURE 4.6: Win rate impact of "open-ended diagnosis"

In call after call, we found average performers missing cues that the customer just wanted somebody to *tell them* what they should buy and instill the confidence they needed to move forward. And, in almost every instance, the net result was the customer saying they "need to think about it some more."

Conclusion

We know from chapter 1 that valuation problems—that is, how to value alternative choices—is one of the three sources of indecision that plague customers and is something sellers must contend with if they hope to get their customers across the finish line.

The social science shows us that excessive choice can overwhelm customers for a whole host of reasons. It can overwhelm because lots of choices means the probability of making a bad choice goes up. It can overwhelm because it leads to feelings of purchase regret—perhaps because they worry that they settled by making the choice they did or maybe because they believe they would have made a better choice had they just waited a bit longer and really thought things through. And it can overwhelm because it is, ultimately, the customer's choice . . . and if it doesn't pan out, they have nobody to blame but themselves.

High performers combat this source of indecision—by making powerful and personal recommendations to the customer, using a combination of proactive guidance and advocacy. Doing this lowers the burden of choice for the customer. The fear the customer has that they're making the wrong choice is addressed by the seller telling them that they're making the right choice or making a choice that other customers have been happy with. Similarly, the fear that they are settling or that they could have waited and made a better choice is put to bed by the rep confidently pointing out the right option, the best configuration, and the ideal package for the customer. And the concern that they will be left holding the bag because *they themselves* made a poor decision is assuaged by the rep personally advocating for a specific choice—"If you're not completely happy with this choice, you can blame me . . . but I know you'll be happy with it."

As compelling as the idea of making a confident recommendation is to salespeople, it should come as no surprise that after decades of training and coaching telling us to do the opposite, most reps—when seeing customers struggle with valuation problems—instead ask the customer what they want, defer to their preferences, and focus on diagnosing and reacting to their needs. In the end, this leaves the customer no closer to solving their valuation problems than they were when they first expressed their confusion about what to do.

In the next chapter, we'll explore the second source of customer indecision, lack of information, and share our findings as to how high performers cope with the customer's desire to do endless research.

CHAPTER FIVE

Limit the Exploration

It's perfectly normal for a customer to want to do their homework—especially when the solutions they are considering entail some amount of cost, risk, disruption, or behavior change on their part. But how much information is "enough" for a customer to make a decision? A good rule of thumb is the "P = 40 to 70 rule."

This concept was coined by General Colin Powell, former chairman of the Joint Chiefs of Staff and US secretary of state, who wrote and spoke extensively about leadership principles over his career. "Use the formula P = 40 to 70," Powell explains, "in which P stands for the probability of success and the numbers indicate the percentage of information acquired. Once the information is in the 40 to 70 range, go with your gut." In Powell's experience, making decisions with less than 40 percent of the information required is just guessing, and waiting until you have more than 70 percent is just delaying. "Don't take action if you have less than a 40 percent chance of being right," he says, "but don't wait until you have enough facts to be 100 percent sure, because by then it is almost always too late. [E]xcessive delays in the name of information-gathering breeds 'analysis paralysis.' Procrastination in the name of reducing risk actually increases risk."[1]

But as compelling as this guidance is, logically speaking, salespeople see customers violate it all the time. High performers we interviewed pointed to excessive requests—for instance, additional demos with the identical stakeholder group and requests for multiple reference calls and proposal iterations—as signs that the customer is seeking certainty before making a decision. The irony, of course, is that customers likely *know* they'll never be able to consume all of the information out there or achieve complete certainty before they make their purchase decision, but it often doesn't stop them from trying. At some point, the customer has enough information to make an informed decision. The question then becomes whether the customer also realizes that this point has been reached.

So what do high performers do to keep their customers from endlessly spinning their wheels?

Our analysis of sales conversations reveals three skills that high-performing salespeople use to limit the exploration: owning the flow of information, anticipating needs and objections, and practicing radical candor.

Owning the Flow of Information

Perhaps the biggest part of overcoming the customer's desire to do more research is for the seller to own the flow of information. The salesperson's objective isn't to prevent the customer from doing research on their own—after all, how could they?—but more to establish themselves as a subject matter expert and a trusted guide to the customer on their learning journey. Doing so sends the message that the customer is dealing with somebody who knows a lot more than the customer does about the product or service the customer is considering purchasing. It shows the customer that they personally don't need to do more research because the seller has already done it *for them*, ultimately helping the customer relax and feel like they're in good hands. For high-performing sellers, it's all about preventing customers from spinning their wheels trying to become experts themselves.

We identified a few tactics for owning the flow of information in our research. First, high performers in our study were far less likely to cede control of the conversation to others inside their own organizations. Specifically, we found that top sellers relied less on subject matter experts like solution engineers, product leaders, and customer success managers in their calls than did average performers, who tended to bring in subject matter experts much earlier.

We ran this finding by some high-performing salespeople and their perspective was eye-opening. "We have tremendous experts across our organization," one rep told us, "but the minute I bring those folks into a call, I start to erode the customer's perception of *me* as an expert. It's like the old saying goes, 'You get delegated down to the person you sound like.' I always want my customers to see me as the source of information and a subject matter expert. If I abdicate that role, they'll only see me as a glorified admin and then they'll start relying on their own research rather than looking to me as a guide and trusted advisor. So, I try to be really choosy about when and where I bring in somebody else." One sales leader we spoke to put it simply: "If you can't speak credibly about the product and need somebody to help you do it, you're not providing a lot of value to me as a customer and I'm not going to look to spend time with you."

Second, we found that when high performers *did* bring in other experts, the percentage of time they allowed those experts to speak during sales calls was orders of magnitude lower than on similar calls run by average performers. A top sales rep in the manufacturing sector explained how she leverages subject matter experts: "It's important to know when you are too far over the tips of your skis and you need to bring in somebody who's deeper on the topic or question the customer wants to discuss. If you don't know the answer, the last thing you should do is fake it. But when I bring these folks onto my call, we always have a prep call during which I tell them exactly where in the conversation I want them to jump in and I make sure that they know they are to hop in, answer a question or provide their perspective, and then hand the reins back to me. That way, the customer sees me as the person who was able to find the resource to answer their questions, not the person who was over her head and needed to hand the discussion to somebody else."

She also explained that she does her best to learn the answers to these more complex questions so that she doesn't have to rely on a subject matter expert the next time around and is able to carry the conversation more of the way to the finish herself. "I take a different approach than most of my peers. They tend to just punt to the subject matter expert right after introductions are made and let that person run the call with the customer. Nothing could be worse for your own credibility and, what's more, our subject matter experts also hate when they do that because it puts the job of selling on their plates when it belongs on ours."

Third, we found that, early on in the sales process, high performers were more proactive than their peers in suggesting additional reading and sources of information the customer should consult to help them come down the learning curve—and, importantly, these were often *not* their company's own marketing materials or thought leadership content. On one call, for example, a top rep laid out a reading list for his customer: "I find that many of my customers go online and try to 'self-educate' around this technology but there's so much content out there that it can be really overwhelming and people just end up confused at a higher level. I'm going to send you a few links to some pieces that I always recommend to people looking at this technology for the first time. There are a couple of articles and a podcast which I really like in which an industry analyst explains—in layperson's terms—how the technology works, what the different use cases are, and what to watch out for when you're evaluating vendors. I'd encourage you to just spend a little time with this content and pass it along to others on the team. I think it will help get you to the 201 level quickly so that you can get down the learning curve and start asking the more important questions you need answered."

Obviously, the ability of a sales rep to offer a compelling and informed point of view on the decision the customer is wrestling with is something that is honed through experience. But lest new salespeople—or those selling for a new company—feel that this is too high a bar to hit, top sellers, in our interviews, admonished them to think differently. One high performer said that the most important thing a new salesperson can do is invest the time to develop expertise on their company's products, those of their competitors, and the market as a whole. She said that when she joined her new company, she found there was a culture of salespeople letting solutions engineers do all of the demos: "The company I came from was one where all salespeople did their own demos. So it surprised me when I arrived here—a company whose product is *less* complex than the one I used to sell—and nobody knew how to walk a customer through the product. I told my manager that I wanted to do my own demos and, after some debate, he relented. I invested a lot of time early on in becoming as good as a solutions engineer in walking a customer through the product. Once others saw the success I was having, they started to come around."

Another tenured rep said that he always encourages new hires to "remember their source of authority": "We sell to CFOs and it's natural to feel intimidated when you're selling to somebody who's been doing this job for longer than you've been alive, but here's the thing: they may know more about being a CFO, but even our least-tenured rep knows a ton more about our product and this technology than any prospective customer. New reps just need to remember that our customers aren't looking for us to teach them how to do their jobs, they're looking for us to help them be smart consumers of a technology they don't know much about."

Owning the flow of information is a critical skill and one that can be used by even less-experienced reps to limit the exploration and help the customer avoid going down "blind alleys."

Anticipating Needs and Objections

The second key behavior that enables reps to limit the exploration is their ability to anticipate needs and objections.

Before we talk about anticipating unstated needs and objections, however, we should first address how best salespeople deal with stated needs and objections. In fact, one of the starkest contrasts we saw in the data was in the way that high performers and their average-performing peers engage customers in the moments that the customer expresses an objection. Objections are an unavoidable part of the sales conversation—in our study, we found that an astounding 69 percent of sales calls contained some form of customer-stated objection. This is particularly true in the simple, transactional sales calls in our study, which are predominantly situations in which the customer *could have* purchased on their own but chose nevertheless to call in to speak with a salesperson. Their decision to call is typically rooted in the fact that they're hung up on some sort of objection, so it's not surprising to hear these come up with regularity. In more complex sales, objections are no less prominent, though they tend to come up later in the sales process as customer indecision starts to creep in and customers weigh the magnitude of putting ink on a contract.

And here a curious gap arises. Rebuttals are indeed common when objections are raised—showing up in 52 percent of sales interactions. But that's seventeen points *lower* than the frequency of objections. A lot of explicit objections simply go uncontested—something that is an absolute conversion rate killer (see Figure 5.1). As a reminder, the average win rate for sales interactions in our study was 26 percent. The presence of objections was one of the

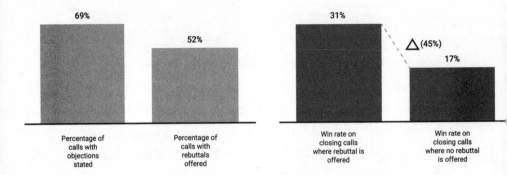

FIGURE 5.1: Frequency of objections and rebuttals;
impact of rebuttals on win rates

biggest drags on conversion, and yet, with just one rebuttal win rates go up to 31 percent. When no rebuttal is offered, conversion rates drop by nearly half, to 17 percent.

Beyond simply meeting customers' stated objections, our research shows that high performers will sometimes anticipate an objection to be coming and preemptively offer a rebuttal—a "pre-buttal," if you will. High performers are always on the hunt for signs of "implicit non-acceptance"—that is, when a change in tone or a slight pause on the part of the customer tells them that something is amiss and the customer's not buying it. In many cases, we found high performers picking up on small signals from the customer—for instance, rather than saying, "Got it," the customer says, "I think so"—and then stopping the dialogue to do a gut check on whether the customer was tracking with them. "I'm sorry for asking," one talented rep said, "but it seems like maybe that didn't resonate with you? I'd love to get any concerns you have on the table so we can have an honest conversation about it. The last thing I want is for you to feel uncomfortable with any element of our offer."

This active listening for signs that the customer is starting to waver turns out to be remarkably effective. In our study, we saw a 40 percent win rate—which was well above the average—when high performers preemptively offered a rebuttal (i.e., offering a rebuttal even when no objection has been expressly articulated). One explanation for why this works so well is that a preemptive rebuttal suggests the salesperson really *gets* what the customer is wrestling with—that they've been there before and have seen other customers struggle with the same decisions. In effect, it makes the customer feel less alone in their indecision.

Make no mistake, picking up on these subtle cues requires exceptional active listening skills and a trained ear. But it also requires a level of comfort with tension that most sellers lack.[2] The vast majority of the time, we found the customer offering signals that they were getting cold feet, and, instead of stopping to root out the cause of their indecision, the seller just kept plowing ahead with their pitch. In many respects, it's human nature to avoid bringing up bad news. But high performers showed a remarkable lack of trepidation in opening the Pandora's box of customer concerns, fears, and objections. Instead, they dove right in. High performers were unafraid to probe when they sensed customer hesitation—knowing that an unstated objection has just as much potential for derailing a sale as a stated one—and, once objections were surfaced, they displayed a high level of comfort in openly disagreeing with the customer, pointing out misunderstandings or putting misplaced concerns to bed.

A sales manager we interviewed in a logistics company told us that this ability to anticipate needs and objections is one of the things that sets her best sellers apart from the rest: "There's nothing more confidence-giving than when a salesperson says, 'I'm guessing you're wondering about X' or 'You know, one of the common concerns I hear at this point is Y.' When you're a customer evaluating a service like ours, it can be pretty scary and overwhelming. We're almost always coming in and replacing a homegrown or legacy process and there are so many different vendors out there now offering platforms like ours. It's head-spinning for a customer. It can be a huge relief for them to know that their concerns are normal and reassuring to hear the salesperson anticipating those concerns."

Practicing Radical Candor

The third behavior that enables a salesperson to limit the exploration is their ability to practice radical candor with the customer.

"Radical candor" is a term coined by former Apple and Google executive Kim Scott in her excellent book by the same name.[3] In it, she explains that there are four engagement styles that a manager can use with their employees, but here we will apply the same framework to interactions between reps and their customers and think about how each applies specifically to limiting the exploration (see Figure 5.2).

The two dimensions Scott lays out are "challenging directly" and "caring personally." The first engagement style is "manipulative insincerity." These reps care more about themselves and what's in their best interests and, rather than delivering honest and direct challenges to customers, they maintain silence and acquiesce to the customer's requests. These are the salespeople who smile and nod when the customer asks for additional information, has follow-up questions, or makes specific requests for more data to inform their purchase decision—and then immediately start bad-mouthing the customer to their colleagues as soon as

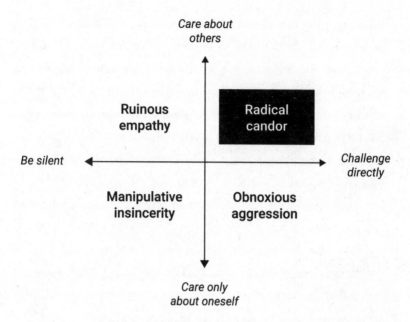

FIGURE 5.2: Four engagement styles[4]

the call is over. One manager we spoke to said that one of the sellers on her team is notorious for this: "He'll immediately get off of a call and talk about how the customer is asking for another demo or an additional reference call and what a waste of his time and the customer's time it is . . . but, ironically, he never shares that view with the customer."

Scott calls the second engagement style "obnoxious aggression." These reps have no problem challenging their customers directly, but it comes from a place of self-interest, not what's in the customer's best interests. This is probably the style most closely associated with the classic, pejorative image of the rude, pushy salesperson. "There are some of these folks on every sales team," one CSO told us. "They are always over-selling the capabilities of our solution and pitching customers on additional add-on services that they really don't need." In the sales calls we studied, this was an easy approach to identify. These reps tended not to *limit* the exploration but rather to *lay waste* to the exploration. They would ride roughshod over customer questions and requests for more information and, when they did acknowledge the customer's request, they tended to do so in a belittling manner that made the customer feel sheepish about even having asked the question or made the request in the first place. For these reps, the "right answer" was always for the customer to buy more and buy it now. And the moment a customer showed the slightest hesitation, these reps were also the first to break out the FUD tactics.

The third engagement style is one Scott dubs "ruinous empathy." Here, the salesperson cares deeply about what's best for the customer, but they're too afraid to share their views with the customer for fear of offending them or rocking the boat. A salesperson we spoke to in our research likened these reps to the Relationship Builder in *The Challenger Sale*. "They really care about their customers and want to do whatever they can to make the customer happy—including things that, deep down, they know aren't really in the customer's best interests. But, they won't bring it up because they fear that introducing any tension into the relationship could bring it to an end." Listening to these calls, you could sense these reps *wanted* to say something to the customer about how the request they were making wasn't a good spend of their time—that it would lead to the customer spinning their wheels and getting no closer to a decision than they were at this moment. Yet, they said nothing.

Finally, there is "radical candor." This is the sweet spot, as Scott explains. Salespeople who practice radical candor are focused on what's best for their customers and aren't afraid to tell them when they're headed in the wrong direction. These reps are unafraid to tell a customer when they're wrong or when they're about to make a mistake. In our research, we found that they were professional but firm in telling the customer that what they were asking for wasn't necessary or that the additional data they were seeking wouldn't resolve the concerns they were hoping to resolve. On one call, a sales rep in an SaaS company told her customer—who was asking for yet another demo—that she didn't think this was a good use of anybody's time. "The last thing I want to do is waste your team's time and, I have to be honest, another demo isn't really going to show you anything that we haven't already showed you. But I also know that you aren't ready to move forward so let's talk about why that is and what I can do to help you make the best decision for your organization—whether that's buying from us or going in another direction."

The above example illustrates an important point: using radical candor to limit the exploration is more than just "calling a spade a spade" and telling the customer they're wasting their time. Reps who use this approach *always* followed it up with a series of questions to dig into what was really motivating the customer's request. This technique bears similarities to the "Five Whys" approach first pioneered by Sakichi Toyoda as part of the Toyota manufacturing process.[5] Toyoda famously advocated for always asking "why?" five times to get to the root cause of a problem.

Unlike average performers who are perfectly happy to indulge a customer's superfluous and unnecessary information requests, high performers look to understand what's driving the customer's request—knowing that there is likely some sort of implicit objection, some form of uncertainty driving the request, and that these requests for additional information are more of a delay tactic than anything else. So, any additional information they can provide won't *really* address the customer's underlying concern. Therefore, they ask the question behind the question to understand what exactly the customer is concerned about—what is driving their specific request.

Time and again, we heard star sellers asking customers to articulate the reason behind their request—an attempt to get the customer's concerns out on the table so that they could be discussed and dealt with. "Absolutely, we can set up a customer reference call for you," one seller said, "but, before I do that, can you help me understand what you're looking to validate in the call? There might be other ways for us to help address any questions or concerns you might have." Another rep told her customer, "I understand you want to hear this from another customer to give you some confidence that you'll see the results you're hoping for, but, respectfully, can I ask you a question? If you hear from our customer that they achieved the results you're hoping to, is that going to be enough for us to get this deal done or are there other things that are giving you pause about this decision?"

And, as we learned in chapter 4, they didn't *just* probe for what's driving the customer's request for additional information; they proactively recommended better and more efficient ways to address the customer's concerns. On one call, for example, a rep asked his customer why they were looking to do another reference call with a different customer organization: "If this is what we need to do to give you the confidence you need to move forward, we'll do it. But I am also concerned that another reference call—which, candidly, is going to be pretty similar to the ones you've already done—isn't really going to address the concerns you have. If you can help me understand what the team is concerned about, I can let you know what the best way is for us to address that." On another call, a rep probed for why the customer was asking for certain data to inform their decision and then, once she felt like she'd correctly identified the customer's hang-up, made a recommendation on a different course of action: "Ah, okay, got it. So, I don't think another call with our product folks is going to address that concern. I think there's a better way for me to get you what you need."

On the face of it, practicing radical candor can feel intimidating for a salesperson and can seem like the sort of approach that might create unnecessary friction between the rep and customer, but it's an approach rooted in empathy and one that has the customer's best interests—in this case, avoiding an unproductive and frustrating exploration—as the guiding principle.

Two Different Soundtracks

A call with a top seller just *sounds* different. In our study, average performers tended to defer to the customer in conversations— saving their product and market insights for moments in the conversation when customers asked questions. High performers, by contrast, were far more assertive in demonstrating their expertise. Where average sellers waited to speak until spoken to, high performers looked to proactively find ways to share their experience and knowledge with the customer. The net impact of this is fascinating. Contrary to popular belief—and what's typically taught in sales training—high performers actually do *more of the talking* than the customer (see Figure 5.3).

For years, sellers have been taught to do more listening than talking. This is an old notion in sales but one that's experienced something of a rebirth as a result of the content marketing done

	Rep talk time, percentage of interaction
Wins	58%
Losses	52%

FIGURE 5.3: Average rep talk time in wins vs. losses

by conversation intelligence vendors. And yet, we find that the exact opposite is true when looking at win rates. In our analysis, sales reps who won deals talked for 58 percent of the time, on average. In lost deals, reps spoke for 52 percent of the time. Clearly, it matters *what* the rep is saying in these conversations—conversion rates wouldn't be nearly as high were the rep making small talk or filling the call with irrelevant information. But what is clear is that if the rep has expertise and a perspective that is valuable to the customer, they shouldn't shy away from taking the time necessary to share it. This doesn't mean that reps should stop listening to their customers during sales calls. Clearly, being an active listener is part and parcel of great selling. But what's also clear is that reps shouldn't be afraid of being proactive and assertive in demonstrating their subject matter expertise.

But it's not just that the best reps do more talking than the customer; it's the *way* they engage customers that's so surprising. High performers, unlike their average-performing colleagues, are quite comfortable interrupting the customer and talking over them when they feel it is important to get the conversation back

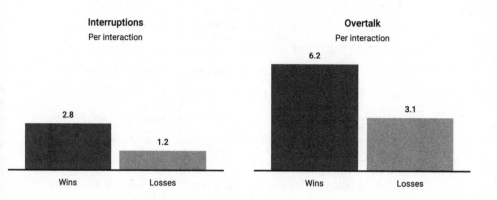

FIGURE 5.4: Interruptions and overtalk in won vs. lost deals

on track. This isn't just contrary to what's been taught in sales training; it feels counter to what our parents taught us about being polite. In fact, we found twice as many instances of the sales rep interrupting the customer or talking over them in *won* deals as compared to lost deals (see Figure 5.4).

While this might seem like rude behavior on the part of the seller, that's not what was going on at all. Instead of impolite overtalk and interruptions, we found that what was happening is what linguists refer to as "cooperative overlapping." This term was coined by Georgetown University linguistics professor Deborah Tannen, who explains that "cooperative overlapping occurs when the listener starts talking along with the speaker, not to cut them off but rather to validate or show they're engaged in what the other person is saying."[6] Tannen says another way to think about cooperative overlapping is "enthusiastic listenership" or "participatory listenership."[7] Others have described this technique as communicating *with* somebody as opposed to *at* somebody, and that not cooperatively overlapping can have the unintended consequence of making the other person feel alone.[8]

This is a critical concept for sellers to understand: listening is important in sales, but if you want to close a deal, engagement is actually more important. Indecisive customers need an active, engaged conversation with a salesperson to get them over the hump. Too often, salespeople see it as more beneficial to defer to the customer, to sit back and listen. And while listening is certainly critical—especially early on in a sale when getting to know the client and their needs—being quiet sends the message that you aren't actually hearing what you're being told. Great salespeople are "all in" on their sales conversations. So, the guidance for sellers isn't that interrupting and cutting off customers will make them buy, but rather that they shouldn't be afraid of speaking, sharing their expertise, and "cooperatively overlapping" with their customers.

There is limited "downtime" in a high-performer sales conversation. When the customer is talking, she is met with verbal acknowledgment while she's conveying her thoughts. We found, quite literally, thousands of instances of the rep saying things like "Absolutely," "Yeah, I hear what you're saying," "Yup, makes sense," "Oh, for sure, I agree," "That's interesting," "Hmm, okay," and many other verbal cues designed to show the customer they are listening to *every word* the customer is saying. And when there are pauses as the customer is speaking, the seller unashamedly jumped in—sometimes to finish the customer's thoughts, sometimes to lob in a question, sometimes to share an example, sometimes to paraphrase what they heard, and sometimes to redirect the conversation.

Before we move on, a quick word about "purposeful silence": this technique, which has been taught to salespeople for years, is one that sellers need to use with care. While it *can* be a powerful technique when used occasionally in a sales call (e.g., asking a targeted question and allowing the customer the time they need to answer it or throwing out a price or term and letting the customer absorb it), our data shows that there is clearly a point of diminishing returns when it comes to silence time (see Figure 5.5). No silence time (less than 8 percent of the call) and too much silence time (more than 30 percent of the call) result in lower conversion rates—likely because too little silence time leaves the customer feeling like they can't get a word in edgewise, whereas too much leaves the customer feeling like the rep doesn't actually know what they're talking about. The optimal amount of silence time is between 8 percent and 17 percent of the call, and is associated with win rates of 30 percent. So, when reps use *some* purposeful silence, it can produce the desired effect. Too much or too little should be avoided at all costs.

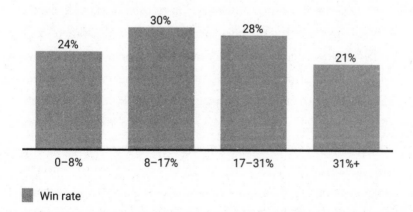

FIGURE 5.5: Sales rep silence time; quartiles by percentage of interaction

In fact, we found that one of the worst things that can happen during any sales call is the "deer in the headlights" moment—that is, when the rep is stumped by something the customer says and struggles to respond. In our model, we found that the combination of rep silence followed by the rep expressing confusion is a toxic combination in terms of win rates.

Conclusion

The data is clear: When salespeople can limit the customer's exploration and keep it within the bounds of "reasonable due diligence," they stand a much higher chance of converting a sale. When reps demonstrate the behaviors we've discussed in this chapter, they convert at a 42 percent rate. On the other hand, when they allow customers to engage in "unchaperoned" and unbounded research, conversion rates plummet to 16 percent (see Figure 5.6).

The customer's desire to seek more information before making a decision is an incredibly difficult hurdle for the salesperson to overcome. Getting them to put their desire to do more research aside requires salespeople to do three things. First, they must own the flow of information. This is about the salesperson positioning themselves as the locus of authority for the customer and not abdicating that role to others in their organization, like subject matter experts or solutions engineers. And, when a rep must bring in additional support to address a customer's questions or concerns, it's about keeping their reliance on those resources to a bare minimum. Second, salespeople must anticipate the customer's needs and objections. Doing so helps customers see that they're talking to an expert—somebody who has been down this path before

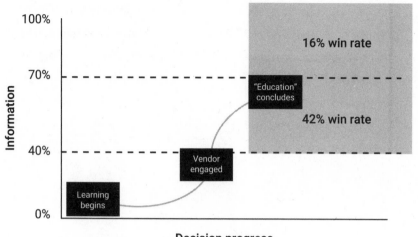

FIGURE 5.6: Win rates for limiting the exploration vs. allowing unbounded research

with other customers and can help them "look around corners" in a way that they couldn't if they were trying to make this decision on their own. And, finally, sellers limit the exploration by practicing radical candor. When customers make superfluous requests for unnecessary data or information, they aren't afraid of "challenging directly," probing for the real reason the customer is asking for this information, and then making a recommendation on a better path forward.

When we compare high-performer sales conversations with those of their average-performing peers, we find that they sound fundamentally different. High performers don't hesitate to share their expertise, they don't allow for "dead air," and they engage in cooperative overlapping with their customers. A high-performer conversation is neither a lecture nor an interrogation. It's an active and engaged dialogue between two equals—a spirited conversation one would expect to hear between two good friends who've known each other forever. More than anything, it feels as if the seller genuinely cares about what the customer has to say and is confident enough to know that the customer will be just as interested in what they have to say.

CHAPTER SIX

Take Risk Off the Table

S o far, we've discussed two reasons that customers need to hit
the pause button and "think about it": a lack of information
and valuation problems. We've discussed where these sources of
indecision come from, how they manifest in sales conversations,
what average performers tend to do when facing these situations,
and what high performers do differently to overcome them.

However, it's the third and final source of customer indecision
that we'll discuss in this chapter—outcome uncertainty—which
sellers often find to be the most intractable and hardest to defeat. Nowhere is indecision as pronounced as it is when customers
fear that they won't capture the benefits they expect from their
purchase.

Even if we are able to convince the customer that they don't
need to do more research, and even if we can help them pick a
good option from a host of what they believe are equally good
options, every customer will still think twice before signing on

the dotted line to contemplate whether they'll actually get what they're paying for. Every buyer has experienced being burned by a vendor or a too-good-to-be-true product description that over-promised and underdelivered. The bad memories of those failed purchases come flooding back and the last thing a customer wants to do is make a decision that will lead to some unforeseen loss. Better to do nothing, the customer reasons, than to intentionally make a decision that ends up costing them.

From earlier chapters we know that average reps respond to the other types of indecision in the way they've been trained. When customers express a desire to do more research, average reps accommodate those requests and otherwise defer to the customer. And when customers struggle with choosing the right option for themselves or for their organizations, the average performer tries to diagnose customer needs by asking probing questions. So, how do average sellers confront indecision that stems from outcome uncertainty?

When faced with this situation—once the proof points, customer reviews, Magic Quadrants, calls with reference customers, and ROI calculators fail and the customer says that they just aren't ready to move forward, and that they are worried about making a decision they'll later regret—the average seller turns to an age-old technique: "FUD," or fear, uncertainty, and doubt.

"We really appreciate all of the time you've spent with us so far. We're sold on the value, but we're going to need some more time to think about it. We're just concerned about our ability to capture the benefits you're projecting," the customer says. With nothing else up their sleeve to pry the customer out of their indecision, the rep looks to sow fear, uncertainty, and doubt in the customer's mind: "I hear what you're saying . . . but I'd hate for you guys to be stuck with your legacy solution and miss out on this opportunity to improve your business." Put simply, the seller's last-ditch effort when faced with outcome uncertainty is almost always to try to scare the customer into buying.

The history of FUD in sales is an interesting one. It's not entirely clear who first came up with the term, but the technique is as old as the profession itself. Maybe older. Sowing doubt in another in order to get what you want was something Shakespeare actually wrote about in the early 1600s. In his play *Othello*, the villain, Iago, after getting passed up for a promotion by Othello, tries to take down his boss and friend by making him believe his wife is having an affair with another man. Roughly one hundred years later, we find the first documented use of the phrase in an essay by the English academic and cleric William Payne. "This will give unspeakable comfort, peace, and satisfaction to his mind," Payne wrote, "and set him not only out of danger and free him from an ill state, but out of all doubts, fears and uncertainties in his thoughts about it."[1] Little did he realize while delivering his treatise on the pros and cons of death-bed repentance that this phrase would become a cornerstone of professional selling in the modern era.

Of course, it wasn't until the 1970s that FUD really became a commonly used technique in sales. IBM salespeople are probably first credited with using FUD to combat an upstart competitor, Amdahl Corporation. Later, in the 1980s, Microsoft became the FUD standard-bearer, using the technique (ironically) against IBM itself. Their objective: to sow seeds of confusion, hesitancy, and skepticism about IBM's OS/2 operating system as compared to Microsoft's Windows 3.1. Even as late as 2010, Microsoft was pushing FUD-based messages to make customers uneasy about open source software, its interoperability with Microsoft's own products, and the lack of available support when things go down. In one video, for example, they warned users: "If an open source freeware solution breaks, who's gonna fix it?"[2]

When we dug into our data set of sales calls, we identified four distinct flavors of FUD that sellers tend to use when relitigating the status quo: urgency, scarcity, wallowing, and isolation. The first flavor, urgency, is a type of manufactured fear based on temporary discounts and special pricing, terms, or conditions. The goal is for the rep to create some angst with the customer, that if they delay the decision, the product or service they are considering may actually cost them more money. Here are some examples from our study:

- "Absolutely, you should think about it some more if you need to. But I did want to let you know that our rates change dynamically and we may not be able to offer you the same pricing if you call us back later."
- "Unfortunately, this is a limited-time offer. We won't be able to give you the same level of discount after this week."
- "My manager had approved this pricing for you based on the assumption that you would sign the purchase agreement this quarter. Unfortunately, I'm not sure I'll be able to get you the same deal next quarter."

The second flavor, scarcity, is about making the customer feel like there is a limited window of time in which to actually get the product they want. It is based on the notion that people value things more when they are hard to get. In his seminal book *Influence: The Psychology of Persuasion*, Robert Cialdini lists scarcity among his "six principles of persuasion." He explains that "when it comes to effectively persuading others using the Scarcity Principle, the science is clear. It's not enough simply to tell people about the benefits they'll gain if they choose your products and services. You'll also need to point out what is unique about your proposition and what they stand to lose if they fail to consider your proposal."[3] Examples we found include the following:

- "We only have a limited number of that product still in stock, and once we run out I can't say when our inventory will be replenished."
- "If you sign by the end of the day, we can pencil you in for an install two weeks from today. Unfortunately, our next open window isn't for another two months after that. That would be a significant time to wait to capture the benefits we've been discussing."
- "I did want to let you know that we've opened registration for our annual event to current subscribers only and it's already almost sold out. We expect it to fill up in the next few days."

The third flavor of FUD is what we call "wallowing." Wallowing is, quite literally, making the customer stew in their own discomfort or discontent with the status quo. When they hear customers start to back away from the purchase decision, reps will often try to remind the customer why they expressed their intention to buy in the first place. By doing so, they hope to dial up the "pain of same" with the customer:

- "I know you and your team are in agreement that the way you do things today is suboptimal. Are you sure you want to continue down that path instead of moving forward with our solution?"

- "I'd hate for you to be stuck with your current platform any longer than necessary given how frustrated you are with it."
- "I hear you that you aren't ready to sign the agreement today, but I'm thinking back to our first conversation when you told me how bad things were. And it's not like you can wish the current situation away."

The final flavor of FUD that we identified was isolation. This is a technique designed to freeze the customer out and make them feel like they are left on an island, alone with the consequences of their indecision, while others make progress. In many respects, this is the harshest of the four because it creates significant fear of potential loss with the customer and also creates feelings of resentment and broken trust, which can backfire dramatically for the seller. We found numerous examples of this flavor of FUD in our calls:

- "I hesitate to tell you this, but our team estimates you guys could lose up to a million dollars by delaying this decision by a quarter."
- "Are you worried about the impact of delaying this platform upgrade on the team? I know you mentioned they are really getting frustrated by the current platform they're using . . . and we all know how hard it is to attract and retain talented staff in this market."
- "As you know, we're already working with all of the other big players in your space. I'd hate for you guys to be left behind here."

Regardless of the type of FUD being applied, we can almost hear the seller's thought process: *Clearly, they must not really believe in how bad their current state is. They must not* fully *appreciate just how much value they're going to receive. They say they do, but they must not believe it. I've got to dial up the pressure so that they see what they stand to lose by not buying.*

The irony, of course, in salespeople trying to use fear to get the customer to buy is that, as we now know, it's fear that is actually *preventing* the customer from buying. And nowhere is this fear more acute than when the customer is worried that they won't capture the benefits they expect from their purchase. This is a big part of why attempts to relitigate the status quo—of which using FUD is a prime example—is actually negatively correlated with close rates.

So, if FUD isn't the right approach, what *does* work?

De-risking the Purchase

In the previous two chapters of this book, we discussed how customers will get stuck for a variety of reasons. Some customers become indecisive because they're afraid of making the wrong choice. When facing this situation, high performers don't ask the customer what they want—they tell them what they need. They simplify the decision by *offering their personal recommendation* based on the customer's specific use case, situation, or needs. Sometimes, customers become indecisive because they are afraid they are making a decision without having done enough research. In these situations, high performers *limit the exploration*, effectively closing off "rabbit holes" the customer could easily head down, eating up time and introducing interminable delays in the purchase process.

So how do high performers overcome the third error customers are fearful of making—outcome uncertainty? Where average sellers lean on FUD techniques to try to scare the customer into buying, high performers know that the real reason the customer is struggling to make a decision *isn't* because they might miss an opportunity to win. It's because they might make a decision that causes them to lose.

Top sellers know that they are effectively asking the customer to take a leap of faith—to trust them that things will be better on the other side of the decision, that money will be made or saved, that risks will be better mitigated, and so on. But pulling them back from the decision is the voice in the customer's head whispering, "Better safe than sorry." The customer reflects on past purchases that didn't pan out and on horror stories they've heard from colleagues and contacts in their network. On paper, the vendor's solution seems like it will clearly make things better, but there's a chance that, despite putting money, resources, and time into it, the results just don't come to fruition. And when that happens, somebody will need to take the blame—and that person is the individual with their name on the contract, the one who lobbied their boss or spouse for the purchase to be made. The costs become very real in the customer's mind, whether that's potentially getting fired or just looking foolish for making a poor decision, and indecision begins to tighten its grip on the customer: *This seems pretty risky . . . and expensive . . . is it really worth it? Better to take a step back and really think about whether this is a smart decision.*

Unlike their average-performing peers who rely on FUD in these situations, high performers have figured out that the way you convince the customer to move forward *isn't* by making the customer feel bad about deciding to walk away from the purchase. It's by making them *feel good about deciding to walk into it.* The star seller's goal in these moments is to instill feelings of confidence, not to sow seeds of regret. They want to make it okay for the customer to say yes now, and they know that the only way to make that happen is to *take risk off the table.*

Set Outcome Expectations

In our research, we were able to isolate three key techniques that high-performing sellers use to de-risk the purchase decision. The first is setting expectations. Average salespeople, more often than not, tend to push gaudy ROI projections from the start of the sales conversation, believing that this will prove irresistible to the customer—or, perhaps, just knowing that customers will often exhibit maximizer tendencies. What they don't realize, however, is that the more unattainable the returns seem to the customer, the more they'll fret about being able to achieve those returns come decision time. High performers focus less on "maximum impact"—that is, what is *theoretically possible*—and more on setting realistic, "believable impact" expectations early on. "We have seen companies like yours realize a threefold productivity increase using our software, but I think we'd be better off managing expectations. I'm extremely confident we'll see *at least* a doubling of productivity since we see that in nearly every customer deployment.

Let's use that to build the business case. Then, when we later beat that figure, it'll be a welcome surprise. Always better to under-promise and overdeliver."

In our analysis, setting expectations had one of the most dramatic impacts on win rates of any behavior we tested in our study. When reps don't properly set expectations, win rates are only 20 percent —six points below the average (see Figure 6.1). (This, by the way, is the norm based on our research.) Reps avoided setting any type of expectation with the customer on 81 percent of calls. But in the rare cases that they did, win rates were nearly double the average, at 51 percent. This represents an improvement of 155 percent, which speaks not just to the stranglehold outcome uncertainty can have on customers but also to the effectiveness of a technique like this to deal with it.

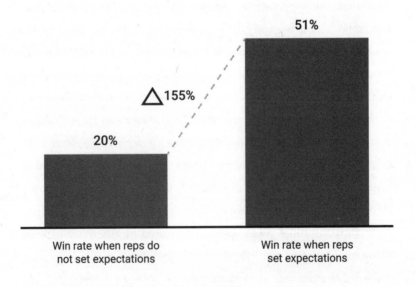

FIGURE 6.1: Win rate impact of setting outcome expectations

Offer Downside Risk Protection

High performers understand that offering the customer a safety net is far more effective than pushing the customer toward the ledge (i.e., using FUD to try to motivate action). If the customer's concern is whether they'll attain the objectives they hope for, they need confidence givers, not fearmongers.

In the sales calls we looked at, we found numerous examples of sellers using creative options to provide customers with a safety net. In the transactional sales calls in our study, this often came in the form of reps making sure customers knew they had a cancellation window, that they could change their plan or subscription at a later date, or that there was a money-back guarantee. "It sounds like you're on the fence," one rep explained, "but let me just assure you that if you decide later that you're not getting the value you expected out of the service, it's free to cancel at any time."

What's interesting is that one would think that offering this sort of assurance to the customer is a no-brainer and something reps would do on a regular basis. Why wouldn't they? If there's even the slightest chance a customer is suffering from indecision brought on by outcome uncertainty, surely it would make sense to proactively mention that sort of safety net to the customer. But, ironically, we didn't find reps relying on this confidence giver very much at all. In all of the transactional sales calls we studied, we found that reps used this less than 15 percent of the time.

Why is this? The first explanation lies in the way reps are compensated. In some companies, reps aren't paid on deals until the customer is out of the cancellation window. Or, perhaps they are subject to a claw-back period during which the company can reclaim sales commissions paid on deals that later back out. The second explanation is that some reps fear that bringing up things like opt-out clauses and guarantees will indicate that they aren't confident themselves in the product or service they're selling and may inadvertently give customers reason to be skeptical. And finally, many reps are so reliant on using FUD to scare customers into action (e.g., "I can't imagine you'd go another day continuing to use the product you're currently using") that suddenly changing course and offering the customer some downside risk protection (e.g., "Don't worry, we offer a ninety-day money-back guarantee in the event our product doesn't work for you") can come off as a bit disingenuous, if not downright awkward.

Of course, in many situations, reps don't have the ability to offer free cancellation windows or money-back guarantees. This sort of thing is a rarity in complex B2B sales, for instance, where vendors invest significant resources into configuring and implementing solutions for customers. So, what can reps do in these situations to offer downside risk protection when their companies don't allow them the latitude to offer something like an opt-out clause? In our analysis, we found that the best reps use a variety of creative confidence givers to help get customers over the outcome-uncertainty hump.

One technique we saw in several calls was creating detailed project plans before the deal closed—with owners, milestones, target metrics, and so on—something that helps show the customer that the rep and her organization know exactly how customers get value out of their offerings. Top sellers often started hammering these out well in advance of signature: "I know we're just starting to work on the contract with legal now and are still a few weeks away from having anything to sign," one rep explained, "but I'd like us to start nailing down the project plan, milestones, owners, and KPIs for the first six months we'll be working together. We built this plan back from the best practices of customers who've seen the best results from their investment, so it's a great road map to follow to make sure you get the value you're expecting out of the platform. We don't want to leave anything to chance."

We also found that top reps relied on professional services support as a way to offer a form of purchase insurance to the customer. One sales leader we interviewed told us that many of his reps shy away from recommending that customers add a professional services component to their agreements for fear that it will give customers the impression that they can't get value out of the solution themselves and will be signing up for a more expensive relationship than they'd bargained for. "But," he explained, "our top reps understand that the bigger concern customers have is not getting the value they expect, and recommending that they add a professional services component to the contract gives them the confidence that they won't be alone on the journey."

Another technique we found that star reps relied on was creative contracting to lower perceived risk on elements of the deal that made customers particularly nervous. One tech industry sales leader we interviewed told us the story of a large deal whereby the customer was about to sign a five-year agreement covering a broad implementation of the vendor's platform across multiple parts of their business. The customer, however, was nervous about the implementation in one specific business unit, which was both their company's cash cow and the implementation that posed the highest number of unknowns given certain legacy systems that had long been in place. At the eleventh hour, the customer started to express concerns about unforeseen implementation problems that might crop up that could negatively impact the business unit's performance. The importance of this particular business unit to the customer combined with the number of implementation unknowns created a sense of outcome uncertainty for the customer and threatened to derail the entire deal.

When no amount of reassurance or executive sponsorship seemed to make a dent with the customer, the sales leader proposed a unique solution: Why not carve out the work for this particular business unit under a separate one-year agreement that the customer was free to cancel at any time? The rest of the contract would cover the implementation for the other business units under the previously agreed-to five-year term, but this one business unit would have an opt-out clause that would help protect the customer in the event that things started to go sideways and they chose to pull the plug. Despite the fact that the overall dollar value went down, the sales leader maintained the previously agreed-to level of discounting as a sign of good faith. He knew his organization would do a great job and swarm any implementation problems that came up, which is exactly what they've done since the rollout began. But the optics of offering an opt-out clause like this helped alleviate some of the customer's concerns that this project might fail in this particular area of their business and that they'd be stuck with it for five years. It made all the difference in terms of making the customer feel comfortable and confident enough to sign the agreement. "By giving a little bit on the initial deal and working to make them feel good about what they were getting into," he explained, "we are paving the way for

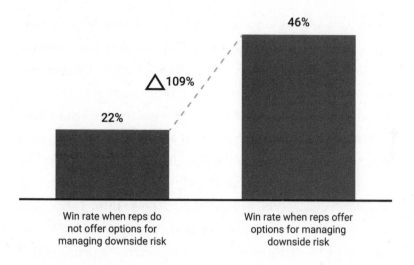

FIGURE 6.2: Impact of offering downside risk protection on win rates

a much more healthy and profitable long-term relationship with them."

The impact of managing downside risk on win rates is significant. In our analysis, we found that when reps offer options that help minimize the perceived downside risk for the customer, win rates jump from 22 percent to 46 percent, an increase of 109 percent overall (see Figure 6.2). Unfortunately, while this is a highly effective technique for battling customer indecision—especially as it pertains to outcome uncertainty—it is rarely used. We found reps doing this on only 14 percent of the calls we studied.

Start Smaller

Finally, similar to something we discussed earlier in the book, we found high-performing reps proactively suggesting to customers that they start smaller than perhaps even the customer wants.

One sales leader we work with whose company provides maintenance services to homeowners and small businesses explained that customers will call up with a whole wish list of things they want to buy (again, maximizer tendencies rearing their heads), and then when they hear the price, they get off the phone saying they need to "think about it." "Our service plan can get pretty expensive when you add all of the various options we offer," he explained. "When the customer calls in and starts asking for the 'Cadillac' package, many of our reps will quote them a price. And when they do, the customer invariably has sticker shock. At that point, it's a losing battle because the rep starts suggesting taking some services off of the order but the customer then feels like they are having to settle and what they're buying is somehow less. But what our best reps understand is that, ironically, they will sell more by selling less." More often than not, this leader explained, his best reps will actually talk customers *out of* additional options before giving them a price—they'll proactively suggest that new customers start with a couple of their most popular services to see how they like them and then offer to follow up in a few months to see if the customer wants to add on to their package at that time. Customers love that the rep is being a good steward of their money and it helps the rep to proactively avoid that sticker shock moment. "Our average reps do the exact opposite," he told us. "Once the customer starts describing this 'all singing, all dancing' plan they have in mind, the rep starts seeing dollar signs and it never even crosses their mind to proactively suggest the customer start smaller."

Another sales leader we interviewed in the wealth management industry told us that when he began his career, he quickly figured out that while he could make more money by pushing clients to go "all in" with him, this dramatically heightened a client's outcome uncertainty. Instead, he learned that it was better to offer multiple options to the client—one "all-in" option, one moderate option, and one "toe-dipping" option. While they would be attracted to the potential returns of the larger proposal, he would proactively steer them toward the middle option as a better way to get started. "Many of my peers back then never figured this out and would instead go 'whale-hunting,' putting only the biggest, most expensive and riskiest proposals in front of their clients because this was, they thought, the fastest way to hit their numbers. But those deals never close and, if they do, the client is immediately second-guessing their decision. Most of those folks aren't here anymore."

This approach stands in stark contrast to what some have argued is the definition of sales success—that anything less than a "high-quality deal" (i.e., a large, high-price-point, long-term, highly profitable deal) should be considered a loss. But the data is very clear: best reps sell more over time and build stronger customer relationships by starting small, not by going as big as they can right out of the gates.

Conclusion

As we've discussed throughout this chapter, outcome uncertainty is arguably the most intractable and difficult-to-overcome source of customer indecision. No customer wants to be left alone, personally accountable for a purchase that didn't deliver the benefits that were promised. Even when faced with a decision that the customer *knows* will make them better off, they avoid making that decision based on even a small chance that it might make them worse off. This is loss aversion in its purest form.

Unfortunately, the way most reps deal with this final mile of indecision is to rely on FUD tactics—an attempt to scare the customer into taking action. But what reps fail to appreciate is that it is *fear* that is driving the customer's indecision, and heaping additional fear onto their shoulders won't motivate them to buy. If anything, it will make them less likely to buy.

Best reps know that dealing with the customer's outcome uncertainty isn't about making them more scared; it's about making them more confident. To do this, they set proper expectations and use creative tactics to minimize the customer's downside risk. Using these tactics can overcome outcome uncertainty and produce dramatic improvements in win rates in nearly all situations, save those cases in which customers are convinced they won't see the benefits of a purchase (see Figure 6.3). In those extreme cases, customers are so debilitated by indecision that the benefits of any purchase are largely ignored—and, more often than not, high performers have already disqualified these opportunities out of their pipelines long before they reach this point.

We've now explored the three sources of indecision—valuation problems, information seeking, and outcome uncertainty—and the approaches star sellers use to combat them, namely, offering their personal recommendation, limiting the exploration, and taking risk off the table.

In the next chapter, we'll consider these behaviors as a whole and look at what makes the JOLT seller truly unique among their peers.

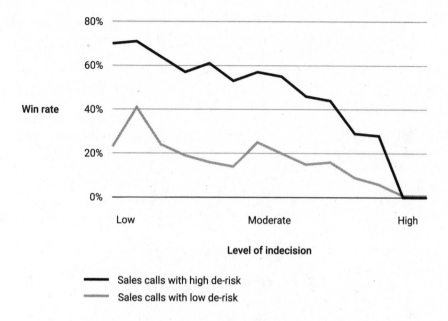

Take Risk Off the Table

FIGURE 6.3: Win rate impact of de-risking skills
by level of customer indecision

CHAPTER SEVEN

Becoming a "Buyer's Agent"

As hard as it may be for the modern traveler to believe, there was a time—not too long ago—when the *only* way to book a trip was by going through your local travel agent. Every town had a travel agency and big cities had one on every block. In many respects, if you wanted to travel, you had few choices for booking a flight other than to call on a travel agent. Only your local agency had access to the proprietary airline booking system required to get you a ticket to your destination. As demand for business and leisure travel grew, so did the number of agencies. From the 1970s to the late 1990s, the number in the US alone ballooned from 12,000 to 45,000.

And then, just as quickly as they came to dominate the market, they nearly disappeared from existence entirely.

The arrival of online travel booking sites like Expedia, Orbitz, and Priceline, as well as the ability of travelers to book directly using the websites of the major airlines and hotel chains, suddenly rendered traditional travel agents obsolete. Almost overnight, travel agencies started closing their doors. In the US, the number of individual travel agents plummeted by 35 percent between 2000 and 2018. Even former US president Barack Obama declared in a town hall meeting the travel agent to be yet another victim of disruption by more agile, direct-to-consumer internet players: "When was the last time somebody went to a bank teller instead of using the ATM, or used a travel agent instead of just going online? A lot of jobs that used to be out there requiring people now have become automated."

But reports of the death of the travel agent had been greatly exaggerated. Unlike other industries that were wiped out by the internet, travel agents have made a dramatic comeback in recent years. The number of independent agents in the US grew from a low of 78,800 in 2018 to more than 105,000 by early 2020. Revenues were also up significantly, with nearly one-third of all trips booked via travel agents. Before the pandemic, the industry was projected to continue to grow by 10 percent per year. And as things return to normal, most industry observers expect travel agents to bounce back—and quickly.

But why would customers suddenly need the help of a travel agent when they have access to an almost limitless amount of information, tools, and resources to research and book trips on their own? Well, it turns out that the resurgence of travel agents has been driven precisely *because* of all the options and information available to consumers. While this abundance may seem like a good thing for customers, it has, in fact, dredged up a host of psychological phenomena that make it *less likely* a customer—even one with a very clear intent to buy—actually ends up buying anything at all.

Consider just one destination, Italy, as an example. A quick search for "Italy travel" yields nearly 2.8 billion results on Google. Paring it down to "Italy travel blog" yields 440 million hits, and "Italy travel itinerary" brings up 33.4 million results. TripAdvisor's "Italy Travel Forum" alone contains half a million topics—some with thousands of individual replies and comments. Amazon lists more than 20,000 Italy travel guides for sale (even narrowing down to only those with at least a four-star rating still yields more than 8,000 books). This is on top of all of the Italian travel content and recommendations available on hotel, airline, and cruise operator websites.

A customer planning a first-time trip to Italy quickly becomes overwhelmed not just with all of the information out there but with all of the options in terms of planning their trip. One well-known expert recommends sticking to a single region so that you can fully explore it while another offers plans for seeing the entire country in seven days. One blogger swears that Tuscany is a must-visit destination and another calls it a "over-commercialized tourist trap." One site suggests a rental car as the best way to see the country and another says that the Italian train system is the only way to go. One says to prioritize Italy's iconic cities—Rome, Florence, Venice—and another advises eschewing the typical Italian destinations and instead discovering the "real Italy" by traveling through the small towns and villages that dot the countryside.

Faced with so much information, so many options, and an endless array of choices, fear starts to gnaw at the customer. They worry that they haven't done enough research—that it was the article or blog they *didn't* read that contained all of the answers they were looking for. They worry about making a selection among so many seemingly good ones. Even if they could make a decision, they know they'll instantly regret passing on those options that they *didn't* choose. And, worst of all, the customer is deeply concerned that they'll make a mistake or a bad choice and it will turn what should be a fantastic trip into an epic disappointment. And they'll have nobody to blame but themselves. So, they may very well *intend* to book a trip, but they become mired in indecision and ultimately fail to act.

Enter the travel agent—or, as they're called today, "travel advisors."[1] When faced with so many options and overwhelmed by the fear of making a costly mistake, today's customers increasingly seek the help of an expert who can help them navigate different options and ultimately instill confidence that the customer is going to have a great experience. More than anything, this is what the curious case of the travel agent—their rise, fall, and ultimate resurgence—teaches us: being a customer in today's world is hard, and overcoming indecision doesn't require a *seller* as much as it requires an *advisor* who can take them by the hand, lead the way, and help them arrive at a successful outcome.[2]

The JOLT Seller: A Buyer's Agent

Anybody who's spent time with a JOLT seller—that is, a rep uniquely gifted at helping customers overcome indecision—can immediately relate to this story. In many respects, it encapsulates the approach these gifted reps take when engaging customers.

In fact, it's no overstatement to say that these talented reps see *the job* of a salesperson differently. Once the customer has agreed on a vision and purchase intent is established, JOLT sellers shift gears and stop *selling to* the customer. Instead—while it seems strange to say—what they do is step in and start buying *for* them. They know that the only reason today's customers have reached out to a salesperson—when they have many options to purchase on their own, without a seller's involvement—is because they are struggling to buy and they need help. The customer may understand *why* they should buy but still require a lot of help with *what* to buy, *how* to buy, and even *when* to buy. Absent that help, there is no hope to overcome indecision and close the deal.

JOLT sellers have an innate sense for the personal role they play in getting the prospect past their indecision. They understand that the buyer needs their help on a very human level. The buyer can't do it on their own. When a customer is stuck, they aren't likely to get unstuck without the sales rep's help. So, rather than continuing to play the role of the salesperson, these star reps assume the role of a delegate—a subject matter expert and trusted partner whom the customer has tapped to help them work through what is contributing to their indecision. They understand that the reason customers often struggle to buy, even after they've expressed their intent to, isn't because they've *decided not to*. Instead, it's because they *can't*. They know the customer's indecision is less a function of something *they did as sellers* and much more a function of *who customers are as people*.

In these moments, customers are looking for a delegate who can help provide them with the confidence they need to ultimately make the purchase. That confidence comes from the prospect being able to air out their hesitancy and a talented seller—a trusted partner—who can guide the customer on what, how, and when to buy. This has the effect of simultaneously improving win potential and easing buyer anxiety, dramatically boosting the odds that the seller will overcome the customer's indecision.

While it makes far more sense for the customer to trust in the seller's expertise—in the same way an overwhelmed trip planner would put their itinerary in the hands of an experienced travel advisor—salespeople know that customers are often reluctant to do so, preferring instead to research options on their own and to double-check that the recommendations the salesperson is making are, in fact, in their best interests. It's not that customers are unintelligent and think that they can become as well versed as the salesperson in the solution being pitched to them. Instead, the reason lies in something called the "principal-agent problem" (also referred to as the agency dilemma).[3]

The Principal-Agent Problem

The principal-agent problem is when one person (the agent) is able to make decisions on behalf of another (the principal), but an incentive misalignment or conflict of interest causes the principal to believe that the agent is making decisions that benefit only themselves. This problem typically arises when there is information asymmetry between the agent and the principal—that is, when the agent has more information than the principal about the decision that's on the table, leading the principal to feel as if something's being kept from them.

Agency dilemmas happen all the time, in both the public and private spheres. For example, clients sometimes distrust their attorneys, who they hired to act in their best interests, because they fear they may just be bilking them for additional fees or perhaps accepting settlement terms that aren't really in the client's best interests. Similarly, economist Steven Levitt shared in his book *Freakonomics* his extensive research into agent-principal problems as they present in real estate transactions. Levitt found that Realtors sell their own houses for more than they sell their clients' properties—an average of 3 percent more, or $10,000 on a $300,000 property.[4] This is largely because, when selling their own homes, they're willing to play the waiting game until they get a good offer (Levitt found that Realtors leave their houses on the market ten days longer than they do their clients') but have no incentive to do this with a client's home since the marginal benefit of getting a client a slightly better offer is nominal to an agent who is only making, at most, 1.5 percent of the purchase price on the deal. As a result, Realtors often convince their clients to accept lower offers that come in quickly, suggesting to them that they want to avoid the negative stigma associated with houses that have been on the market for a long time.

But perhaps nowhere is the agency dilemma more apparent than in the relationship between sellers and customers. In almost any sale, the balance of power is tilted toward the seller. Customers don't know what they don't know when it comes to a supplier's offerings. The seller, on the other hand, knows what customers really need and what they don't. They understand where the land mines are that need to be avoided. They know which capabilities are real and which are more conceptual. They know the experiences happy customers have had and those that have led to churn. They know where the bodies are buried. The customer can get insight into *some* of these things by consulting user reviews, analyst reports, and third-party purchasing consultants, but they'll never acquire the level of knowledge that somebody who works in the supplier organization possesses.

Then, when you add in the fact that the seller is incentivized to convert the customer and drive up the dollar value of the deal as much as possible, it's a recipe for a classic agency dilemma and a lack of trust between the two parties. Fearful that they may have missed something, and skeptical that the seller has shared all of the information they need to make a good decision, the customer—rather than going with their gut and just making a decision—will instead opt to do more research and request more information from the seller, all the while thinking that it's the *next* piece of information they consume that will allay all of their concerns.

So, what can salespeople do to overcome the agency dilemma and establish the trust necessary for the customer to put themselves in the hands of the rep—to trust that this person isn't just a *salesperson* but is a *buyer's agent*?

Overcoming the Agency Dilemma

In our study of sales calls, we identified several techniques used by high performers that help overcome the agency dilemma. One of the most impactful was suggesting that the customer not "overbuy" where they don't need to—an idea we also discussed in the previous chapter. Customers will often come in looking for a more expensive product or service than what their specific needs demand, and it represents a prime opportunity for the seller to develop trust and demonstrate credibility by suggesting the customer spend *less*, not more.

In one insurance sales call, for example, the seller told a customer who was debating whether to add supplemental coverage to a new policy that, in his opinion, the customer already had sufficient coverage and could save some money by not increasing it. The customer was effusive in her praise for the rep: "Thank you so much. I really had no idea how much coverage we should be carrying and I appreciate the fact that you didn't try to sell me more than I need." The customer then proactively asked about whether she could save even more by moving her other insurance policies over to the company—in the end, leading to a much larger bundled sale for the rep. And, similarly, in one software sales call we studied, the salesperson recommended to the customer that he consider scaling back the number of licenses he was putting in the initial contract: "You know, if I were you, I would take the number of licenses down from ten to five. Start smaller with a core group of power users and let's generate some demand for expanded usage across your team. The last thing we want is for you to feel like you spent money on licenses that are going unused."

Another technique for building trust and overcoming the agency dilemma is offering positive feedback on a competitor's offer or even outright recommending a competitor's product or service as a better fit for the client's needs. In one transactional sales call, the customer referenced a better price point offered by a competitor for what seemed like an identical service plan. "That is a great price for that plan and I wouldn't blame you for taking it. We do offer better coverage and we think we provide superior customer service, which is why our price is a little higher." And in another sales call involving a more complex purchase, a confident rep went so far as to recommend a competitor's solution over her own company's offer: "Honestly, if you guys are really focused on that particular use case, I would tell you to talk to our competitor. They're the market leader in that space and they make a great product. If you think your needs will expand beyond that use case, however, we think we're the better partner given our ability to serve other parts of your business. Still, I don't want to mislead you into thinking we're just as good as they are in that particular area because we aren't. It's just not where we've focused our development efforts."

By the same token, we found best reps freely admitting that their company's product or service can't yet do everything the customer is looking for. Too often, average performers claim that their company's product can do anything and everything the customer is asking for—which is a surefire way to generate customer skepticism (after all, what vendor's product does it all perfectly?) and, in the unlikely event the customer actually believes the rep, can sow the seeds for future churn when the customer later realizes they've been oversold. Best reps are comfortable indicating where capabilities aren't fully developed or are future road map items. In one call we analyzed, the rep said, "We don't actually offer real-time analytics yet. We think our solution is fast enough for practitioners—and offers the deepest level of insight on the market—but real-time is still on our road map. We're working on it but I don't want to overpromise here. It's unlikely we'll have that capability for at least a year."

Finally, a small but impactful way to build trust and credibility is when reps openly admit they don't know the answer to a question. This isn't to suggest that it isn't paramount that reps demonstrate expertise—it absolutely is. But, at the same time, a well-timed admission that the customer's question is one they can't answer helps the customer to see that the rep isn't trying to railroad them into a purchase that may not suit their needs. One in-bound sales rep in our study said to a customer, "You know, I don't actually know if our product integrates with that system. I've never been asked that before and I don't see anything in our knowledge base about it. I can certainly find out, however."

These sorts of proactive suggestions—that the customer not overbuy, that a competitor's offer might be better for the customer's needs, that certain capabilities aren't ready for prime time, or that the rep doesn't have all of the answers the customer is looking for—help customers see that the seller is *on their side*, not an adversary to do battle against but a trusted advisor to collaborate with. When coupled with the JOLT behaviors we've already discussed in this book, it's a powerful recipe for overcoming not just the sources of customer indecision but also the agency dilemma that can stand in the way of consummating a deal.

When "Yes" Is the Easiest Choice

When reps execute this playbook at a high level, they earn the right to confidently ask for the business and make "saying yes" the default option.

In their popular book *Nudge: Improving Decisions about Health, Wealth, and Happiness*, Richard Thaler and Cass Sunstein explain that humans are governed by two "systems" of thinking.[5] The first is the "Automatic System," which is "rapid and is or feels instinctive and it does not involve what we usually associate with the word 'thinking.'" This system is often associated with reflexive actions—pulling one's hand away from something hot, flinching when hearing a sudden loud noise, and even saying "excuse me" when bumping into somebody inadvertently. The second they call the "Reflective System," which is more deliberate and is typically associated with "thinking." We use the reflective system when deciding what to eat for dinner, what movie to watch on Netflix, what options package to choose for our new car, and whether to accept a new job offer. It is within this second, Reflective, system where indecision happens—when customers fret about whether they've done enough research, whether they've made the right choice, or whether they'll get the benefits they hope for—and it's a sign that they are reflecting and thinking critically about the decision in front of them.

Thaler and Sunstein found that an effective way to nudge people toward a decision is by offering something called a "default option." Defaults work because they turn what would normally be deliberative choices into instinctual ones—in other words, they take decisions off of the reflective track and put them onto the automatic one. Why? Because a default represents the path of least resistance; it taps into our desire to conserve energy. In other words, picking something other than the default requires energy that we'd rather not expend. But, more importantly, a default serves as an implicit recommendation that is being made by a trusted authority. Clearly, somebody smarter than we are chose this as the default option—and they have our best interests in mind—so who are we to disagree?

A good example of a default at work is when companies automatically enroll employees in their 401(k) plans, which has been shown to boost participation rates from less than 50 percent (when employees have to opt in) to more than 90 percent (when employees are automatically enrolled and have to instead *opt out* if they don't want to participate).[6] Another example of a default is placing healthy foods at eye level in a cafeteria—customers could select unhealthy options, but they would have to make more of an effort to get them.

Confidently asking for the business works the same way for salespeople. At once, it positions saying yes and signing the agreement to move forward as the default option. Saying yes becomes the easy choice whereas saying no feels like a hard gearshift, a break in the forward momentum, and an undesirable change to what has been a smooth process. Asking for the business is also the rep—who has already established herself as a trustworthy and credible expert—making a recommendation to move ahead with the purchase. For salespeople, this simple technique is the equivalent of taking the customer by the hand and saying, "You sound ready to me. Let's go." Like a skydiving instructor stepping up next to a nervous first-timer at the threshold and giving that last boost of confidence that nudges the student to take the leap, it's a powerful moment in the sales conversation. In many cases, it seems to stop the customer in their tracks and gets them to buck up for the final step in the process. Customers, we found, will rarely immediately reply to the rep's request with their invoicing or billing information. Instead, the reply is more often along the lines of "You know what? Yeah, I think I'm ready. Let's go ahead and do this."

We saw many flavors of this in the calls we studied:

- "If you're good with what we've discussed, let's go ahead and get this order processed for you. Can I have your permission to go ahead and submit it?"
- "We're excited to bring you on as a customer and start delivering the benefits we discussed. I'm going to send over the agreement. Once we have it back, we'll be ready to go."

- "I'd like to get you on the calendar for implementation and onboarding. Should we go ahead and get things rolling? If you're in agreement, I can send you the DocuSign right now."
- "This is a great choice for your business. I'd say we should go ahead and get it locked in. I can take your credit card information whenever you're ready."

In many respects, there is nothing more central to being a salesperson than asking for the sale. However, it often surprises sales leaders when they learn that their reps do this far less often than they think (or hope). In our study, reps actually asked the customer for the business only 46 percent of the time. This means that in more than half of all sales conversations, not only is there no confident close, but there's no actual discussion of a sale at all. But sales leaders would be misguided by assuming that the "fix" to this issue is to get their sellers to ask for the business on every sales call. The more accurate interpretation of this finding is that in more than half of sales opportunities, salespeople haven't earned the right to do so.

Conclusion

Having demonstrated deep knowledge and expertise with the customer, top sellers turn their attention to ways in which they can establish trust and thereby overcome the agency dilemma that is endemic to the customer-salesperson dynamic. While average sellers have grown up believing (or being taught) that they should never admit that a customer doesn't need everything they think they do, that a competitor's product might be a better fit, that certain capabilities aren't quite ready for prime time, or that they just don't know the answer to one of the customer's questions, high performers do the exact opposite.

In the next chapter, we will consider how JOLT is a recipe not just for improving win rates but for building long-term customer loyalty for the organization.

CHAPTER EIGHT

Beyond Win Rates: JOLT-ing Customer Loyalty

S ales leaders are increasingly pushed by their CEOs and executive peers to deliver healthy, profitable growth, not just a focus on customer acquisition at all costs. For the business, the goal isn't just to convert sales. It's to build long-term customer loyalty. While this begins with the initial conversion, those wins either become amplified through continued purchases, increased spend, and positive word-of-mouth or they become customers who churn out, feeling burned by their experience and sure to share their negative sentiment with others.

This book is full of examples and ideas sellers can use to JOLT past buyer indecision and win more deals now. But this isn't just a story about improving win rates. It's also a story about improving the customer experience, setting up the rest of the organization for ongoing and sustainable success. For example, we detailed in chapter 3 how high performers recognize the maximizer tendencies of highly indecisive customers and aim to set realistic, "believable impact" expectations, especially early on in relationships. This is an important sales behavior that eases the decision process, builds trust, and softens buyer uncertainty around outcomes. But it is also important to other people across the enterprise whose job it is to care for and expand a new customer relationship over time. Think about the account manager or customer success manager who is tasked with maintaining and renewing that relationship. Or the customer support and service reps who are asked to address post-sale issues and reset expectations that may have been mis-set during the sales process.

The Four Flavors of Customer Loyalty

Walt Disney once remarked, "Whatever you do, do it well. Do it so well that when people see you do it, they will want to come back and see you do it again, and they will want to bring others and show them how well you do what you do." It's a great way to describe what loyalty is all about: products, brands, and experiences so differentiated and compelling that customers happily buy them, demand more of them, and encourage others to become customers too.

A few years ago, our research team developed a framework to explain how to think about the drivers of customer loyalty (see Figure 8.1). According to our research, loyalty has two dimensions. On

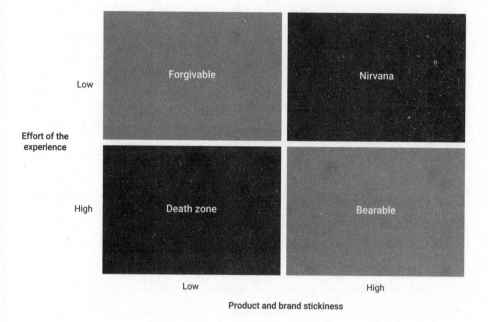

FIGURE 8.1: Four flavors of loyalty

the one hand, there is the "stickiness of the product or brand," ranging from low to high. This is about how embedded the product is in the customer's life or business and how difficult it might be for a competitor to dislodge or displace you as the preferred supplier. On the other axis is the "effort of the experience," also ranging from low to high.

Readers will intuitively understand product and brand stickiness. Some products are so compelling and differentiated— because of how advanced or sophisticated they are, how well designed they are, how cool they are, or maybe just how inexpensive they are—that we gravitate toward them. And other products and brands are the opposite, so we are constantly on the hunt for something better.

The vertical axis, "Effort of the Experience," draws from research in *The Effortless Experience: Conquering the New Battleground for Customer Loyalty*.[1] The crux of this research is that, when it comes to the post-sale experience, excessive friction and unwanted effort can create customer disloyalty. Effort can come from a whole host of things: confusing marketing messaging and pricing information, hard-to-install and hard-to-use products, and clunky customer service interactions. The research clearly shows that customers who have low-effort experiences are far more likely to renew their relationships with companies, much more likely to spend more, and much less likely to spread negative word of mouth about brands. Low-effort experiences are also far cheaper for companies to deliver since ease translates not only into less work for the customer but also less work for companies. Easy experiences don't translate into unnecessary break/fix requests, repeat contacts, long service calls, expensive truck rolls, and so on.

Obviously, the best place to be is in the upper right, where companies deliver compelling, differentiated, and sticky product and brand experiences *and* deliver a low-effort customer experience. Only a handful of companies and products fit here. For many consumers, Apple devices or Amazon Prime are perfect examples—they're incredibly sticky products that offer great value propositions and are remarkably easy to use, even when things go wrong. Despite continual price increases, most customers barely think twice before paying significant premiums for Apple products or re-upping their Prime subscriptions regardless of the price increases Amazon continually applies.

And, of course, the place to avoid, in the lower left, is the "death zone," where companies deliver difficult, high-effort experiences and offer an undifferentiated, uncompelling product or brand experience. This is the lose-lose box of loyalty where customers experience high amounts of effort but see no reason to stick with a brand. For one cable company we worked with, we heard a customer spend fifteen minutes explaining to a rep that he'd already spent roughly twelve hours combined trying to fix the issue he was having with his wireless router. He spent hours on the company's website. He went to the router manufacturer's website. He went to YouTube and various online support communities. He had called a half dozen times over the course of three days reexplaining his story every single time he called. "You guys are WASTING my time," he screamed, and then went on to threaten canceling, moving to a competitor (a competitor, he noted, that offers the same internet speed for less per month), and telling everybody he knows not to do business with the company. That's what the lose-lose box feels like and, unfortunately, we can all think of a handful of companies that fit in that zone.

While there are notable examples of companies in the upper right and lower left, the reality is that most companies fall into the other two zones, which are more nuanced. The upper left quadrant—low effort with low brand stickiness—is one we call "forgivable" because it represents those companies that earn customer loyalty *strictly* because they're easy to work with, not because they make or deliver anything of any particular value. Your neighborhood grocery store might be a good example. Other stores may offer a better selection, better prices, and so on, but if it's 5 p.m. on a busy workday and you need a quick, nearby dinner option, the local grocery store almost always wins out. For others, their bank or credit card company might fit the bill. There are probably better options out there—banks or cards that offer lower rates and more perks, more appealing branches or slicker mobile apps—but yours is good enough and it's not really worth the time to switch.

The bottom right quadrant we call "bearable," which is for products that are hard to use but are nevertheless compelling and sticky. Some might consider, as an example, an expensive luxury car that, despite being a headache to maintain, is really fun to drive, so the customer puts up with it. Or maybe it's your local coffee shop that has spotty Wi-Fi and surly baristas but makes the best coffee around. In some cases, companies that fall into this zone have "captive loyalty" relationships with their customers. Despite the high level of effort these types of brands deliver within the customer experience, customers still feel relatively captive because switching is just too costly or annoying. Think about the airline you normally choose when you travel. When you're a few flights away from earning the next loyalty tier, you will probably put up with a few extra flight cancelations, inefficient boarding processes, or unhelpful customer service calls. Or maybe your cable company fits here: you feel like you overpay for slower internet speed and fewer channels than what the competition offers, but you can't bear the thought of switching, dealing with another installation appointment, and returning your old equipment. You are, in every sense of the word, "stuck" with these companies.

But what does any of this have to do with sales and with the JOLT research, in particular?

Winning Now, Losing Later

Sales organizations—perhaps more than any other part of an enterprise—are extremely outcome-driven. Leaders, managers, and sellers are typically incentivized to max out quotas and hit numbers within defined periods of time. Given that, salespeople might be quick to dismiss the idea of building long-term loyalty as "somebody else's problem."

But what happens if indecision exists (and remember, it exists in at least moderate to high levels in 87 percent of sales opportunities), and the seller does not employ JOLT behaviors but is nevertheless able to wrestle the deal across the line? As we have discussed at several points across this book, indecision—even if it is overcome during the sales process—can linger long after the contract is signed. This phenomenon—when people reevaluate their decision *after* it's been made—is what psychologists refer to as "post-decision dysfunction." "Indecisive individuals," writes researcher Eric Rassin, "may worry about several topics even after they have come to a decision. For example, they may wonder whether their choice was the best possible one. Alternatively, they may worry about their decision-making strategy: Did they do it the right way? Did they take all of the necessary steps in the decision process?"[2]

Rassin talks about three types of post-decision dysfunction: worrying, checking, and decision instability.[3] These are all relatively straightforward and very typical in situations in which a customer doesn't feel confident in their decision—perhaps because they felt rushed at the end or they remain uncertain about how to enact the change or that there's something about the offer that doesn't sit right with them—but they make a decision anyway. When that happens, you can bet that customer still feels a high amount of effort, and one of the obvious outcomes is to start fretting about whether they made the right call or made a mistake. In his own research, Rassin and his colleagues found a significant correlation between a person's indecisiveness and their tendency to worry about a decision after having made it.[4]

Beyond simply worrying about whether they made the right decision, some customers will take the extra step to start checking their decision-making work. This is when customers go back and do more research about options, *after* the decision has been made. They start consulting more reviews, they look through other vendors' websites, and even consult subject matter experts and purchasing consultants—despite the fact that they've already signed an agreement to move forward with a company's offering. The fact that indecision leads to checking one's work has been documented in a wide range of studies, including Randy Frost and Kenneth Sher's study of why certain students recheck their answers and take longer to turn in their exams than others. Their conclusion: dysfunctional post-decision behavior rooted in indecisiveness was to blame.[5]

The final behavior associated with post-decision dysfunction is decision instability. This is, quite literally, when a customer changes their mind and chooses a different option from the one they originally selected. As Rassin explains, "Individuals who are indecisive may be less convinced of the justness of their conclusion and may therefore tend to alter it if faced with new information."[6] Salespeople are very familiar with this tendency. Customers who express hesitancy and who need to be wrestled across the finish line are often the same customers who later recant their decisions—invoking cancellation clauses and asking to be let out of their agreements.

How JOLT Reduces Customer Effort and Post-decision Dysfunction

As part of our study, we were able to measure the specific relationship between customer effort and sales win rates (see sidebar "How We Measure Customer Effort"). Though win rates will differ slightly based on context and situation, it's clear that increased effort makes a seller's job much more difficult in converting sales (see Figure 8.2).

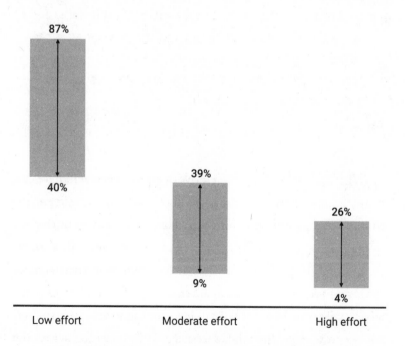

FIGURE 8.2: Win rate range by level of customer effort

HOW WE MEASURE CUSTOMER EFFORT

A few years ago, the research team at Tethr developed a way to measure the level of effort a customer perceives in a service interaction based on the raw conversational data (e.g., a recorded phone call, chat interaction, or email exchange). Based on more than ten years of research on the drivers of customer loyalty, the Tethr Effort Index (TEI) is a deep-learning model comprising more than 280 variables that effectively predicts what customers would answer on a Customer Effort Score survey question (i.e., "How easy was it for you to get your problem resolved?").

Tethr research indicates a strong correlation between TEI scores and other predictors of customer loyalty such as Net Promoter Scores and Customer Satisfaction. In our research, we found that TEI also proved to be a strong predictor of sales win rates.

When buyers perceive high levels of effort, sellers will have difficulty attaining even average levels of performance. Moderate levels of effort can still pull win rates as low as 9 percent. But, when sellers are able to keep effort levels low, win rates range between 40 percent and 90 percent. The evidence is clear that high levels of effort and friction hurt conversion potential. What's more, the approach practiced by most sellers—attempting to relitigate the status quo when the customer shows signs of indecision—actually increases customer effort (see Figure 8.3).

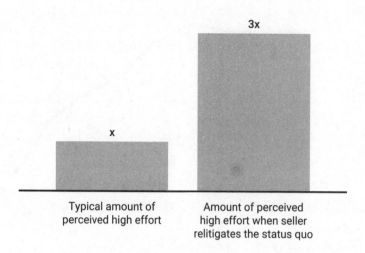

FIGURE 8.3: Effort impact of relitigating the status quo

Relitigating the status quo after intent is established only heightens current fears—by wallowing in that pain, isolating decision makers, or scaring buyers about inaction—and fails to address growing personal concern around post-purchase chaos. In contrast, JOLT is a way for sellers to work *with* their customers, addressing the fears that are driving their indecision. Our data clearly shows that as sellers increase their use of JOLT behaviors, customer effort levels decline precipitously (see Figure 8.4).

Why does using JOLT make the sales experience *easier?* Recall that what buyers fear most is their own personal role in taking action. Now, imagine the relief that a buyer—guarding against repeating past mistakes, asking for extensive amounts of information—feels when the salesperson shuts down unproductive explorations, or the clarity that a personal recommendation can provide, or the protection one feels when offered a small but

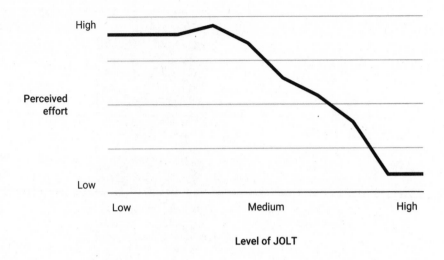

High

Perceived effort

Low

Low   Medium   High

Level of JOLT

FIGURE 8.4: Impact of JOLT behaviors on customer effort

meaningful safety net that helps de-risk the decision. Pain reduction is a very personal activity. It is perhaps the most human of things a sales rep does. High-performing sales reps use JOLT as a way to reduce buyer-perceived pain and, in so doing, lessen customer effort that can lead to future disloyalty and churn.

As individual behaviors are broken down and examined within the lens of customer effort, it also seems clear that sellers are rewarded for at least *trying*. Even regrettable behaviors we'd normally associate with underperformance, such as misdiagnosis or expressing confusion, seem to be only mildly annoying to the customer when compared with other behaviors we'd associate with unhelpfulness. JOLT behaviors like setting expectations are especially powerful both in overcoming indecision and in reducing effort. This may speak to the fact that buyers expect some degree of effort but are especially turned off by unexpected effort.

Conclusion

For the seller, it's difficult enough to get any buyer, gripped by indecision, to transact. As we've demonstrated at length throughout this book, JOLT is the best way to win more business in the face of customer indecision, representing a hugely important new playbook for salespeople, sales managers, and sales leaders. The way most sellers handle indecision—relitigating the status quo—backfires, in large part because it actually *increases* customer effort. This experience then leads to post-decision dysfunction, which can have a widespread, negative downstream impact. And that's a problem that spans far beyond the sales organization. JOLT-ing customers past indecision reduces customer effort, enriches the customer experience, and significantly improves the odds of building long-term, loyal customer relationships.

This brings to a close our discussion of the JOLT method—what it is, why it works, and what it looks like when deployed by salespeople. Across the remainder of the book, we'll take a deeper dive on some of the enablement questions that leaders will have about the approach as they think about how to embed it within their organizations—starting with how to size the indecision problem for a sales organization and assess the level of JOLT capability across the sales team.

CHAPTER NINE

How Much Is Indecision Costing You?

If you've read this far in the book, it's probably safe to assume you recognize indecision as a problem—whether for you personally, for your sales team, or for your company. But what you probably don't yet know is the size and scope of the problem and whether to invest the time, energy, and resources to fix it. In this chapter, we'll introduce some practical approaches to assessing the impact that customer indecision has on an organization, both at the aggregate level and at the individual seller level.

Sizing the Indecision Problem for a Sales Organization

Before we talk about how to assess reps, it makes sense to think about how a sales organization can determine whether it has a customer indecision problem at all. For some sales leaders, they'll just know it in their gut—that more deals than they'd like end up slipping, or perhaps that a higher percentage of deals than what is acceptable end up going radio silent. But for those unwilling to make this assessment on instinct, there are multiple data sources that can be used to scope and size the indecision problem a company may be grappling with.

Perhaps the most obvious choice is CRM data. When using this, it makes sense for leaders to first establish what is an acceptable "lost to inaction" rate for their company. In our study, the average percentage of deals lost to "no decision" was anywhere between 40 percent and 60 percent, depending on the organization. This represents an undeniable and significant deadweight productivity loss for the average sales organization. Objectively, we feel the number should be significantly lower than that for a high-performing sales organization. But, the dynamics of every industry and every market are different. One sales leader we interviewed in the B2B SaaS market, for instance, said that theirs is a tightly defined market and that, over the years, they've sold to every company in their prospect pool. So, almost by definition, they have a huge percentage of deals lost to inaction every year. "I'd kill for a 40 percent percent 'no decision' rate," he told us. "For us, it's more realistic to shoot for bringing the rate below 60 percent since it's an order of magnitude higher than that today."

The other consideration in establishing a "hard deck" for deals lost to indecision is establishing sales cycle times by deal type and customer segment. Large deals sold to enterprise or government customers will invariably take longer to close than smaller deals sold into the mid-market or SMB segment. Similarly, products and services sold to individual buyers will vary in sales cycle depending on price, contract length, and other factors. Figuring this out is critical so that sales leaders know what the "age out" date is on deals—that is, the point beyond which deals can be considered stuck.

One other way that CRM data can be leveraged to assess the overall indecision rate is by looking at interaction frequency. Research by Challenger has shown that healthy deals show a higher velocity of interactions between customers and sellers—that is, when emails and calls happen at a greater frequency, it's a signal of deals nearing closure, whereas deals that have interactions happening at wider and wider gaps as time progresses are more likely to end up lost or in no-decision-land.[1]

Once a benchmark is established within the sales organization, managers need to understand the performance distribution across their sellers. Like anything—tenure, conversion rate, bookings, deal profitability, and so on—leaders will likely find a normal distribution of performance. Some sellers will have a far higher rate of deals lost to inaction and some will have far lower rates, but the majority will cluster in the middle. As we'll discuss more in the chapter on coaching, the tendency of most sales managers will be to focus their coaching energy on the tails—those with the highest rates of deals lost to inaction (because they represent a huge productivity loss for the organization) and those with the lowest percentage of deals lost to inaction (because these reps remind managers of themselves). But, research by CEB (now Gartner) showed that coaching is most effective when targeted at the middle of the sales force: "Left to their own devices, sales managers often skew their coaching efforts toward the tails . . . [But] the real payoff from good coaching lies among the middle 60 percent—your core performers. For this group, the best-quality coaching can improve performance by up to 19 percent."[2]

One final thought on assessing the organizational impact of indecision is that companies should establish this as an ongoing metric in their quarterly business reviews. Only looking at win rates to determine what and who is selling effectively can be misleading since it lumps together two types of loss that have inherently different root causes. Deals that are lost because the customer says no—whether, for instance, the product isn't a great fit, a competitor has offered a more compelling proposal, or the buying committee couldn't reach consensus—is a fundamentally different problem to solve than deals in which the customer says yes but *still* doesn't buy. More often than not, this is a sign that sellers have failed to bridge the gap between intent and action. This is not a product-market fit problem, a value proposition problem, an insight or messaging problem, or even a problem of failing to execute the company's established sales process. It's a seller skill problem. Namely, it's an inability of sellers to effectively overcome customer indecision. Put simply, treating lost deals as all the same creates serious blind spots for managers, which can then lead to a misdeployment of scarce resources as well as manager time—and, ultimately, a failure to solve the real problem.

Once companies have established their own baseline and wrapped their heads around the nature of the size and scope of the indecision problem their organization is grappling with, the next step is to understand how indecision affects sellers at an individual level.

Assessing Individual Sellers' JOLT Skills

As we will discuss in the final chapter, sales organizations should tune their sales hiring criteria to start screening for JOLT-ready reps. But what about the existing sales team? How can leaders assess the capabilities of their individual sellers to understand their performance profile as it relates to JOLT skills in order to identify areas for improvement? Clearly, the answer lies in being able to assess our sellers—but how do we do that effectively?

Throughout the rest of this chapter, we'll explore three different approaches companies can use to get a handle on the current level of JOLT skills among their salespeople, ranging from low-tech to high-tech: manual call auditing, customer surveys, and conversation intelligence. Each can be a viable approach to assessing JOLT skills, although each has pros and cons, which we'll discuss in more detail in the coming pages.

Taking a Manual Approach to Sizing the Indecision Problem

Today, the default approach to assessing seller skills is frontline sales managers sitting in on sales calls or listening to recorded calls by their reps to understand what they're doing well and where they can improve. In large-scale inbound call centers, this task is usually owned by a quality assurance team that will audit a sample of calls from each rep each month—with scores feeding not just rep performance evaluations but also development plans and manager-rep coaching sessions.

On our website, **www.jolteffect.com**, we've provided a sample call-auditing tool that managers can use to score a rep on their use of JOLT techniques on an individual sales call or with a specific opportunity. While manual call auditing certainly has the lowest start-up cost (since it requires no additional technology investment), it is also the most labor-intensive, and one of the hardest to get right. Over the years, we've worked with numerous companies to overhaul their current call-auditing processes and have seen a variety of mistakes companies make that can undermine the benefits of such an approach.

First, there is the small sample size nature of call auditing. In a large-scale inbound sales call center, the industry standard for call auditing is usually 1 percent of total call volume. In an outbound sales organization, this percentage tends to be higher (since the call volume is much lower), but it's still typically a small percentage of all the sales calls an individual rep will conduct. Furthermore, it's rare that a manager will audit *all* of the conversations across a given sales pursuit. In companies where sales cycles are measured in months or longer, a manager might sit in on or audit only a small fraction of all the interactions pertaining to a specific deal. Since small samples are obviously less representative of overall performance than large samples, there's a much higher probability that manual audits surface false negatives and false positives—that is to say, small sample size audits run a much higher risk of incorrectly diagnosing a rep as being either lacking in a certain skill area or demonstrating strength in a certain skill area. Obviously, a way to control for this is by increasing the sample size, though this approach quickly runs into management bandwidth constraints, which is why, in large-scale inside sales groups, companies often look to use a dedicated team, typically quality assurance (QA), to do the auditing work.

Second, many manual call-auditing efforts end up being based on criteria that are binary or rote, meaning managers start looking for specific phrases or utterances being used rather than broader competencies being demonstrated. This leaves little room for interpretation by reps who would otherwise prefer to tailor their approach to a specific customer or situation. This is a particularly acute problem in large-scale call centers where QA teams are auditing hundreds or even thousands of calls a year and calls need to be assessed quickly in a "tick box" manner or the work won't get done. Best companies equip their call auditors (whether frontline sales managers or QA) not with scorecards that ask whether a certain skill was demonstrated but with competency-based scorecards that ask auditors to specify the level at which a certain skill was demonstrated, from novice to expert or mastery level.

Third, manual call auditing is typically an exercise in which managers are looking for a whole host of things for reps to demonstrate—not just JOLT skills but other skills they've been trained in as well as customer, product, or industry knowledge. Additionally, sales managers or QA teams are often asked to listen for compliance issues or customer feedback on new products and offers as well as competitive mentions. Going through a call while simultaneously listening for so many different things obviously increases the risk that something will be glossed over or missed entirely. For this reason, many companies with large-scale call centers will split up their QA teams into those auditing calls for skill and competency demonstration and others auditing calls for things like compliance, competitive mentions, and market feedback.

Any company relying on a manual call-auditing approach needs to seriously consider how they are addressing these issues lest the effort—and the investment made—end up being for naught. Failing to address these issues obviously blunts the impact of coaching that would stem from such efforts but also runs the risk of disengaging reps who may come to see the process as unfairly arbitrary and penal (given small samples or binary scoring criteria) or simply not helpful to improve their craft and drive better results.

Using Structured Customer Feedback to Size the Impact of Indecision

In most large-scale sales call centers, QA scoring is coupled with post-call survey feedback to round out the performance picture. Similarly, outbound sales organizations will often rely on win-loss surveys and interviews to try to learn not just why a customer chose to buy or not to buy but also what impact the salesperson had on the outcome. In the same vein, a company can (and should) supplement any manual call-auditing process with a voice-of-customer approach, like a survey, to capture the customer's assessment of how the rep performed and perception of the overall experience.

When properly deployed, post-sales surveys and interviews can be a solid tool for companies to better understand the impact that indecision may have had on a specific deal. Like manual call auditing, surveys are not without their own problems, however. Principal among them is the low response rates they tend to earn from customers who are bombarded by surveys from all suppliers.

Like the sample size issues related to manual call auditing, small sample size surveys also can lead to false positives and false negatives, which can negate the intended development benefits of the approach.

Another shortcoming of surveys is that customers will often provide quantitative feedback (i.e., they will answer questions that have simple response scales, like "strongly agree" to "strongly disagree") but are typically far less likely to provide detailed qualitative comments, leaving managers scratching their heads as to why customers gave the scores they did. Here, win-loss interviews can be a more valuable approach—although it is worth noting that they are certainly more time-consuming and labor-intensive and suffer from a different form of sample bias, in that most or all of the respondents are wins rather than losses. Without detail from losses, it becomes much more difficult to understand indecision.

Like call auditing, managers looking to use surveys or win-loss interviews to understand the impact of indecision on an opportunity and to assess sellers' JOLT skills will find themselves jockeying for precious and scarce real estate with others—in sales, product, marketing, and so on—who are looking to use the survey as a vehicle to answer their own pressing questions. The straightforward answer, simply adding more questions to the survey, is not an option, typically, given the negative correlation between survey length and response rates. The more questions companies add, the more likely customers will bail out part of the way through rather than completing the entire instrument.

Readers can download a set of survey or win-loss interview questions that can be used in a post-sales setting from our website, **www.jolteffect.com.**

Using Conversation Analytics to Gauge the Impact of Indecision

For sales leaders and managers looking to improve the performance of their sales teams, one of the most exciting developments has been the advent of machine learning–based conversation intelligence. These platforms—which include Tethr, the platform our team used to do the research for this book—represent a step-function change in the way companies assess seller skills, understand the experience they're delivering to customers, and spot opportunities for targeted coaching.

As described on page 5, a conversation intelligence platform takes recorded sales conversations—whether from a web conferencing platform like Zoom, Teams, or Webex, or any of the dozens of call recording platforms used in inbound sales call centers—transcribes the audio into text using automatic speech recognition software and then allows practitioners to mine the data for insights. Given the shortcomings of manual call auditing that we discussed earlier in this chapter, it comes as no surprise that there's been an explosion of interest in this new technology and its potential for shedding light on what's long been a dark data asset for companies. Once companies can "listen at scale," they can capture new insights not just into the performance of their sales reps but into broader questions of customer experience, sales effectiveness, marketing campaign and offer resonance, product performance, and compliance risk, to name just a few. Recorded sales conversations represent an incredibly rich data set for companies to tap, allowing them to finally break free from traditional methods of customer insight collection, such as surveys, which are increasingly characterized by low response rates and thin verbatim.

Still, while the market has seen an explosion in the number of providers of this technology and interest level is high among sales leaders, the attach rate remains very low—according to the research firm Aberdeen, only 26 percent of companies have adopted conversation intelligence. And from our own research at Tethr, we estimate that nearly 80 percent of companies that *have* deployed it also report that the investment failed to deliver its intended ROI. In a series of more than one hundred in-depth conversations with early adopters of this technology—spanning multiple industries—our team identified a few pitfalls of conversation intelligence investments that practitioners need to be mindful of before they head down this path:

- Difficulty extracting insights
- Inability to effectively action against insights
- Prohibitive total cost of ownership

For the remainder of this chapter, we'll delve into each of these pitfalls in detail and, in so doing, help companies avoid the missteps of their predecessors and capture the intended benefits of their conversation intelligence investments.

Difficulty Extracting Insights from Voice Data

By far, the most common complaint of early adopters is that it's too hard to get insights out of their conversation intelligence platform. This challenge presents in many ways. First and foremost, users lament the fact that, using their conversation intelligence solution, they can do little more than spot keywords (e.g., looking for every time a rep uses the word "price" or a customer mentions a specific competitor by name), which, even if captured accurately, fails to—by itself—deliver real insight into where sales efforts are breaking down and what companies can do to address it. Keywords, these companies learn, provide little more than proxy insights, and without fully understanding the context of the conversation, these proxies often prove inaccurate and unreliable.

To get deeper insights out of transcribed calls, companies must use "categories." A category is a machine learning training set (also called a "topic" by some vendors). Rather than simple keyword-spotting, a category is a bucket of phrases or utterances that together describe a specific concept or behavior. Think about, for instance, some of the seller skills we identified as part of "taking risk off the table"—like managing expectations or providing downside risk protection. Each of those seller behaviors can be demonstrated in dozens or even hundreds of different ways by an individual salesperson. A category is therefore a collection of all of the relevant phrases and utterances that could indicate a rep is managing expectations or providing downside risk protection to a customer.

Most conversation intelligence platforms come with a number of out-of-the-box categories, although those tend to be simple customer sentiments (e.g., frustration, confusion, price concerns) or rep behaviors (e.g., acknowledgment, probing questions).[3] At present, no platform would come prebuilt with JOLT categories (aside from Tethr, which is the platform we used to do the research for this book). That said, nearly any conversation intelligence platform has the ability to build customized categories, and there is no reason a company couldn't invest the time and resources to add this to their existing system. However, building entirely new categories can end up being extremely resource-intensive, costly, and time-consuming. Companies typically find that to do this sort of work, they need either to rely on their own in-house data science capabilities or hire the vendor to do the work for them, which can lead to expensive statements of work and professional services fees (only to find that software vendors may not be optimally positioned to find and construct sales behaviors found in conversation data).

Another reason early adopters have struggled to get actionable insights out of conversation intelligence is because they rely too heavily on tonal sentiment analysis. Sentiment is typically gauged in two different ways in a conversation intelligence solution: tonal sentiment (whereby the system picks up voice inflection patterns to determine a customer's sentiment) and syntax-based sentiment (whereby the system looks at the actual words being spoken to determine a customer's sentiment). While tonal sentiment has come a long way and continues to improve as a technology, it tends to yield a high percentage of false positives—for instance, believing a customer is angry when, in fact, the customer is calling from a mobile device in a crowded space and is just speaking loudly so that she can be heard. Additionally, many syntax-based sentiment models rely on traditional keywords, which can often lack the nuanced context necessary to recognize more complex emotions (an important component in understanding how sellers handle different levels of customer indecision).

Finally, companies have been frustrated by the fact that insights remain trapped in their conversation intelligence platform, creating "insight bottlenecks" in the organization. This happens in a few different ways. For one, leaders will purchase a conversation intelligence platform for a sales-specific use case (e.g., assessing and coaching reps on selling skills) but find that the platform they purchased isn't something that can easily be used by other functions (e.g., product, customer experience, marketing) to address their own insight needs because, ultimately, it is purpose-built for a single use case. In the end, the sales department is forced to play the role of "insight help desk" for the rest of the organization. A related issue is that companies often find that the insights from their conversation intelligence solution are hard to distribute to other platforms or systems (e.g., CRM, business intelligence, and reporting tools), again trapping valuable insights inside the sales organization rather than disseminating them for broad consumption across the enterprise.

In an all-too-familiar refrain, one customer we interviewed told us, "We still have one year left on our existing conversation intelligence contract, but we decided to shut the platform off. At the end of the day, it was too much work to get the platform to yield any kind of actionable insight that we could confidently act upon."

Inability to Effectively Action Against Insights

The second most frequently cited pitfall in our study was the inability to drive action—or, more simply, to "move the needle"—on a company's key business priorities. Every company goes into a conversation intelligence investment with a set of key objectives they are looking to deliver against for their organization. In sales, these objectives might be lowering the percentage of deals lost to inaction, improving rep adherence to the sales process, boosting upsell and cross-sell effectiveness, and so on. Depending on the functional area, of course, these objectives can vary. Marketers, for instance, are focused on improving offer effectiveness and gaining competitive intelligence, CX leaders are focused on eliminating customer journey breakdowns and raising Net Promoter Scores, customer success is interested in improving user adoption, and customer support is interested in reducing effort and eliminating friction points from the post-sales service experience. But while all companies we interviewed could crisply articulate the goals they had going into their conversation intelligence investment, far fewer were able to claim victory and point to demonstrable business improvements—even for those organizations who were able to extract insight from the platform to begin with.

In our analysis, we found two key reasons that companies struggle to advance their business priorities when relying on conversation intelligence: first, an overreliance on descriptive, surface-level insights and, second, the lack of a robust customer engagement model that supports companies in achieving the performance gains they're looking for.

In order to truly drive action around insights, a vendor must help a customer generate more than simple descriptive analytics (the "what"). Instead, they must help their customers use analytics to understand the "why" and the "how" behind the "what"—namely, why certain outcomes happen and how to move them in a positive direction. For instance, if a company is trying to move sales conversion higher, it's not enough to know what percentage of the time the rep is talking during the conversation or whether reps are asking questions. Instead, it's critical that companies understand—at a deep level—the way in which specific language techniques, utterances, offers, and so on, affect conversion rate. And they need to understand how changes in these techniques will affect sales outcomes so that they can consistently and predictably move the conversion rate in the right direction. In practice, this means that companies need to look to their vendors to provide not only insight into what's being said to customers but also predictive (correlation) and prescriptive (causal) modeling to guide the right investments in tools, training, coaching, and other forms of sales enablement. To use a simple analogy, if you're finding puddles of water in your house, it's not enough to know that your roof is leaking. Without understanding where and how the water is infiltrating the house—and how to stop it from happening—you can only place buckets on the floor to collect the water. You have no way to address the underlying problem.

Second, companies need help from their vendors to actually leverage the insights coming out of conversation intelligence platforms to drive real change. Companies we interviewed told us that their vendors were good at helping them identify problems in their business—and, in some cases, even helping them recognize the drivers behind the problems and potential solutions—but far less effective at partnering with them to actually drive the change. As one customer told us, "Our vendor only offered to help us drive change with our insights if we paid for an engagement with their professional services group. For cost reasons, we decided to go it alone and ended up stepping on numerous avoidable land mines that derailed our improvement efforts. It was like they had a secret road map for success but wouldn't share it with us unless we paid for it."

In short, companies in the market for a conversation intelligence solution need to guard against the high probability that they will be unable to drive change with the insights they surface. Avoiding this problem requires that insights are actionable (i.e., that they go beyond the descriptive and instead get to predictive and prescriptive) and that the vendor provides a customer engagement model designed to help companies actually make progress against key objectives.

Prohibitive Total Cost of Ownership

The third and final issue cited by those companies who've adopted conversation intelligence is the prohibitive total cost of ownership (TCO) that the solution often entails. As one executive told us in our research, "I never thought I'd say this, but at the end of the day, it was actually more cost-effective for us to continue to have people listen to calls and look for insights than to use our vendor's analytics package. When we did the math and added up the TCO, it was incredibly expensive."

The TCO of most conversation intelligence platforms breaks down into direct and indirect costs. On the direct side, there are costs related to call ingestion (usually priced per minute) to cover transcription, processing, and storage, as well as seat-based licenses for users. In some cases, typically for premise-based systems, customers will often incur capital costs for hardware and software they are required to buy (which will go through regular replacement and upgrade cycles). These costs are typically laid out explicitly in the vendor's term sheet and contract.

What ends up catching customers by surprise, however, are the many unforeseen costs related to making conversation intelligence work. For instance, most customers find that to do anything more advanced than descriptive analytics and keyword-spotting with prebuilt categories—for example, tuning categories or building custom categories, adding asynchronous metadata or doing predictive and prescriptive analytics—they are forced to either hire their own team of data scientists or hire the vendor's professional services team. This can mean numerous, expensive statements of work just to get insights out of the platform. And, if customers wish to ship data to downstream applications (CRM, BI tools, enterprise data lakes, etc.), they are often required to buy an extract license to get their data out of the vendor's servers. Many vendors will also charge a reprocessing fee for running additional analyses on audio that's already been processed (i.e., when sales leaders want to go back to calls that have already been analyzed to look for different things from what they looked for originally).

Beyond these costs, enterprise leaders in IT, analytics, and procurement are often frustrated to find that their various internal business customers (sales, customer support, customer success, marketing, CX, product, etc.) will each buy a platform that is purpose-built for their needs (as most vendors in this space specialize in analytics for a particular domain area). Not only does this add cost and complexity to the organization, but each of these point solutions will often require that customers pay to separately ingest and process the same audio data into their respective platforms (i.e., the CMO may be double-paying to process audio into his analytics platform since the sales leader has already paid to process the same audio into the platform her team uses). And beyond this, there are the less quantifiable but more nefarious costs related to siloed operations—what happens when different functions are listening to the same customer voice using different lenses of measurement, for instance.

To get a real sense for both direct and indirect costs, companies need to look beyond the term sheet to really understand the all-in costs of a conversation intelligence solution. If a platform is not built with the practitioner in mind—that is, if it is hard for a layperson to quickly and easily turn unstructured voice data into structured data that can be analyzed and studied—the costs can be well in excess of what the customer expected to pay when making their initial investment. Further, if the platform is purpose-built for a specific function or use case, companies will need to be prepared to multiply the TCO several times over as different parts of the organization invest in their own point solutions to analyze customer voice data.

Readers who are considering a conversation intelligence solution for their organization can download a free buyer's guide at **go.tethr.com/buyers-guide-to-voice-analytics**.

Conclusion

Assessing JOLT for an organization happens on two levels—first, a company must understand the size and scope of the indecision problem facing their sales force and, second, individual sellers need to be assessed on JOLT skills to spot areas for improvement and targeted coaching.

When assessing individual seller skills, companies can use a wide range of approaches—from very low-tech (manual call auditing) to very high-tech (conversation intelligence). Each approach has its advantages and disadvantages to consider. In a world in which most companies are trying to eliminate manual tasks and reduce their reliance on low-response-rate surveys, conversation intelligence represents a breakthrough technology for organizations looking to better understand their sales effectiveness and customer experience. Unfortunately, the experience of early adopters hasn't instilled confidence in those companies still waiting to invest in this technology. Difficulty extracting insight from call data, challenges generating real business improvements, and a typically steep TCO all represent real obstacles standing in the way of conversation intelligence platforms delivering on their intended benefits. Would-be buyers need to appreciate and understand the challenges that companies encounter with conversation intelligence investments so that they are savvy consumers of this promising new technology.

In the next chapter, we'll discuss how JOLT applies to different types of sales environments.

CHAPTER TEN

Applying JOLT in Different Sales Environments

As for any new study of sales effectiveness, it's natural to ask how the findings might apply to one type of sales organization versus another. This chapter will examine where those differences may lie and how JOLT may differ based on what you are selling and to whom you are selling.

Before we explore those differences, it's worth noting the extensive common ground we see in the data. All salespeople, in some form or another, sell change. And their job is not just to influence and persuade but to motivate customers to take action—to not only convince the customer that the status quo is untenable, but that change is worth it and their fears about change are solvable. While buyer decisions exist along a spectrum of complexity—where some decisions are simple, less expensive, and purely transactional whereas others are complex, quite expensive, and can involve lots of strategic implications—there are certain common themes that emerged from our analysis:

- Indecision represents one of the biggest drags on win rates irrespective of what we sell or to whom we sell.
- Indecision is rampant and unavoidable—we can't wish it away or disqualify it all out of pipelines.
- Indecision appeared with the same frequency and degree in all of the sales calls we studied. There was no sales model, company, or industry that we could declare to be immune from it.

Consequently, as we examine the JOLT method, we see remarkable consistency across industry, sales model, and purchase complexity. Customer indecision is a universal *human* problem that all sellers must figure out how to navigate.

Having said that, spotting indecision and the JOLT implementation guidance for teams will differ from one sales setting to the next. The most obvious differences lie in how the framework applies to different buyer types. Sellers who sell simple, transactional products to individuals likely face a different set of challenges than do sellers who sell more complex solutions to large buying groups or companies. Across the rest of this chapter, we will explain how JOLT should be applied in these different sales settings.

Inbound Sales Channels

Inbound sales has long been an important channel in consumer industries like financial services, telecommunications, utilities, travel and leisure, insurance, and retail—and the importance of this channel has only grown with the decline in retail foot traffic brought on by the pandemic.

But inbound sales is not a channel unique to B2C. As companies across B2B industries become more sophisticated in terms of what their customers can purchase online themselves—placing not just simple product orders but configuring and procuring sophisticated solutions like cloud computing services—the inbound sales channel serves as a critical "second stop" on the buyer's journey, just like it does in B2C companies. As a result, B2B organizations have become far more aggressive in moving their simple transactional sales to online and inbound "inside sales" channels in recent years. Doing so has allowed them to reduce cost-of-sale and refocus their scarcest resource—experienced field sales reps—on selling more complex, expensive, and difficult-to-sell solutions.

More often than not, by the time any sales rep is speaking to a buyer in this channel, the customer has already done extensive research. They have scoured online reviews, weeded through recommendations, consumed expert reviews and analyst reports, and studied supplier websites to compare and contrast features and benefits across different suppliers. Given how much information is available at the customer's fingertips and how easy vendors have made it to purchase online, it's actually a bit surprising just how many buyers still decide to pick up the phone and call. One would have expected that in this day and age, very few customers—especially those considering simple product purchases—would actively decide to speak to a sales rep at all. But inbound call volumes have stayed stubbornly persistent over the years. In fact, there is some evidence those volumes have and will continue to increase.

Why? Like our travel advisor story earlier in the book, the amount of information available to customers often has the effect of overwhelming them—making them feel not empowered but confused as to what they should do.

Time Is Money

The single most distinguishing factor to consider about sales opportunities in this channel is that, very often, these calls are like an entire sales process shrunk down into thirty to sixty minutes. Consequently, the first thing great JOLT sellers do is make sure the inbound caller is in fact a viable buyer. With so many avenues to conduct open and transparent prepurchase research, let alone make the purchase on their own, the majority of inbound buyers already *want* to buy at the point of that conversation. The very fact that they're calling is a sign of purchase intent. In our data, typically 60–75 percent of inbound sales calls or chats were with customers who expressed clear intent to purchase right at the beginning of the conversation. From the very first moments of the exchange, these buyers were sharing all the homework they'd conducted, detailing comparisons already made, and asking specific buying questions.

What about the remaining 25–40 percent? The answer to that question provides a very important lesson to sellers in an inbound sales organization. As we examined the interactions where intent to purchase was *not* there, we found something surprising: the vast majority weren't actually sales calls at all. Instead, these were customers who had service requests but, for one reason or another, wound up in the sales queue. We found that these misdirected calls happened for many reasons: some callers accidentally keyed in the wrong number, some were former customers who were trying to track down information (e.g., credits, tax information) but were no longer able to authenticate through the automated system, and others selected the sales queue because they knew from prior experience that the company answers sales calls faster than service calls. Regardless of the reason, these service contacts end up creating a significant drag on the overall productivity of an inbound sales organization.

Perhaps not surprisingly, because these customers are not looking to buy anything, these calls result in the lowest sales conversion rates of any of the call types in our study, at only 16 percent. Not only do sales reps not sell very much to customers looking only to get problems resolved, but the calls themselves—while shorter than sales calls—are still time-consuming for sellers. For a large company handling thousands of sales interactions a year, this represents a massive opportunity to free up seller time and redeploy resources.

High-performing JOLT sellers in inbound sales environments see their time as a scarce resource. In our study, we found that these top performers excelled at judging the level of customer indecision. They were far more likely to suggest—typically within a minute or two—that the caller's issue would be better handled by a service representative so that they could get on to the next call in the queue that, ideally, had a potential buyer on it.

Unlike their high-performing peers, average-performing sales reps spend significant time trying to help customers looking to resolve service issues. While their hearts are surely in the right place, the data suggests that they would be better off sticking to sales and passing along service calls to the right department. Salespeople who opt to try to resolve service issues rather than pass them on quickly find themselves out of their depth. The percentage of time sales reps are silent on service calls—an indicator that reps are stumped by a customer request and unsure of how to proceed—is significantly higher than what we see from them when they are dealing with sales inquiries.

Companies we work with sometimes point to the concern that transferring a customer to another department will only create more customer effort and frustration, so better to have a sales rep try to address the issue than pass the customer on to somebody else. But in research we conducted at CEB (now Gartner), we found that one transfer can actually be a net positive when positioned in the right way by the representative ("I want to get you to somebody who I know can solve this problem for you") and when the transfer is "warm," meaning that the sales rep stays on the line until the service rep picks up the transferred call and explains the situation to her colleague.

The bottom line is that judging indecision in inbound channels is about reading signals sent early in the conversation and transferring service-oriented asks in a warm and tactful manner. For callers who represent sales opportunities, the vast majority are coming into the queue with purchase intent already established. So the sales rep's job is less about persuasion and more about motivation to overcome whatever is driving their indecision. And, if that weren't challenging enough, the seller typically has less than an hour to do so (and in some cases far less than that).

Guiding Inbound Callers to Make the Right Decisions

High-performing inbound sales reps—just as in other sales settings—absolutely use personal recommendations to help buyers move past valuation concerns. This is particularly important in an inbound sales environment because the inbound sales rep typically has no way to rely on a previous relationship—no bank of goodwill and trust. To be sure, many factors influence buyer trust—the supplier brand, product demand, third-party recommendations—but all of those are out of the seller's control. This places added pressure on limiting purchase exploration. The medium is constricting, everything riding on the words conveyed here and now—no email to be exchanged over the course of a few months, nor follow-on calls to set up. Time is scarce, the clock ticking until the call or chat disconnects. Buyers are always in a separate location, often with several web browser tabs up in front of them. The seller is very often on a ledge all by themselves, without access to subject matter experts or senior managers to help land deals. And it's far too tempting for hesitant shoppers to just hang up, think more on it, and purchase later. High-performing JOLT sellers, knowing they have no second chances, need to work especially hard to avoid damaging blind alleys. Taking risk off the table also takes on a special nature when the buyer is considering spending their own personal, hard-earned money, as is the case in many sales to small business owners. It's one thing to worry about making a poor purchase for your company—after all, nobody wants to explain something like that to their boss—but it's another thing entirely when the money is coming out of your own pocket.

There are plenty of times when the potential buyer asks for

more time to decide. In our study, average-performing inbound sales reps responded in one of two ways. Either they would deploy a form of FUD, using scarcity or price-driven urgency in an attempt to close the deal now (e.g., "Okay, but I can't guarantee this discount will last") or they would defer entirely, quickly accepting the offer to let the customer call back later. As we already know from our earlier discussions, the attempts to scare customers into buying rarely work, and even when they do, they result in customers quickly feeling regret about their purchase and calling back to cancel. But the other approach is no better, as the customer will rarely, if ever, actually make good on their promise to call back later. Instead, they are just letting the rep off easy, so as to not appear impolite when what they really mean to say is "no thanks."

Knowing this, brands that sell in more transactional settings often hand salespeople certain tools that allay risk. Money-back guarantees, try-before-you-buy offers, free trial periods, and flexible payment terms put in the hands of a salesperson can be a powerful mechanism for overcoming outcome uncertainty. Usage of these tools remains a choice, however—one that too many either misuse or underutilize while the best JOLT sellers deploy them in a judicious and effective manner.

Now that we've discussed differences inbound sales reps face when dealing with buyer indecision, let's shift our focus to outbound channels.

Outbound Sales Channels

Millions of businesses rely on outbound channels to grow, and this remains the dominant sales motion in most B2B organizations today. In the more complex solution sales calls in our study, the majority of the calls were between sellers and prospective customers (i.e., hunting), but we also collected a significant number of calls that were with existing customers—that is to say, from account management teams selling existing clients on renewal and upsell or cross-sell offers (i.e., farming).

The primary distinguishing factor for outbound sales is, of course, that it typically proceeds over the course of weeks, months, and quarters. Entire committees of people get involved and participate as a team on many of the calls across the purchase journey. Prices are generally much higher, contract lengths are significantly longer, and purchases often must run the gauntlet of approvals ranging from procurement to finance, information security, compliance, and legal. Initial customer engagement typically begins far before the salesperson gets involved. A curious decision maker may have downloaded a few white papers and the marketing team works to keep that potential lead warm through a series of targeted emails sent over the course of a few months. Perhaps a technical user attended a webinar a few months back and was added to the newsletter distribution list. Or maybe a handful of key user buyers asked for a demo at a trade show and now have joined an online discussion board that is actively monitored by the vendor's demand-generation team.

Marketing-qualified leads are commonly handed to teams of business development reps (BDRs), who then work the phones and email to further qualify interest and purchase intent. Of course, even if an outbound salesperson has the luxury of a BDR team priming the market and booking appointments for them, most still find themselves searching for buyers in all sorts of places: social media, trade shows, industry events, or good old-fashioned "dialing for dollars," placing calls or sending emails in hopes of catching the right person at the right time with the right offer.

Managing Indecision across the Long-Cycle Sale

Let's imagine the stars align and a seller catches a potential buyer with real need and interest. It's not simply a conversation that ensues but rather, an entire *process*. When considering indecision, this is no small fact. If a customer is indecisive, their indecision will reveal itself across the entire sales process—not just on the first sales visit, nor only on the last, but everywhere in between: in emails, voice mails, texts, Slack messages, and more. Whereas in small business decisions, the buyer might worry about spending too much of their own paycheck on a purchase, buyers in larger businesses fear the wrong decision can end their paycheck altogether. That dynamic will differ based on specific products and services being sold, but in many cases, the old adage that "Nobody ever got fired buying from IBM" still applies. That is to say, customers will often select the safe choice from the proven supplier even if a lesser-known vendor is offering a far better option. The reason is that, in complex solution sales, people get fired for making poor, negligent, and ill-informed purchase decisions.

The most extreme versions of this tend to dovetail with purchases involving very long sales cycles. One company we work with, for instance, sells heavy construction services (i.e., hospitals, stadiums, office buildings, and other large-scale projects). There are thousands of decisions that need to be made between the time the project is green-lit and a shovel is put in the ground—and almost all of these decisions are risky and irreversible. For instance, how big should the lab be in a new hospital? On the one hand, a bigger lab would accommodate future growth and new equipment. But, on the other, a bigger lab may mean a smaller emergency department or maternity ward. Making the wrong decision means living with it for a long period of time. You can imagine customers in this environment experiencing significant valuation concerns and outcome uncertainty.

Those who sell services face a particularly difficult environment, where indecision takes on even thornier forms. In professional services, for instance, a partner is both "salesperson" and the product itself since it's their expertise and experience the client is looking to buy. And that expertise may help the seller when offering their recommendation. But these sellers are also often only part-time sellers, which, of course, reduces the number of repetitions any one salesperson might get in dealing with customer indecision. It may also impact buyer concerns of the agency dilemma problem we discussed at length in chapter 7. On the one hand, if the service relies in part on advice known but not yet given, it's the very definition of an agent withholding key information, increasing buyer desire to conduct more prepurchase research to confirm principal assumptions; on the other hand, the seller's level of expertise should also help limit unnecessary exploration and increase buyer comfort with ambiguity.

A hallmark of high-performing solution sellers is that they don't "chase garbage trucks." Instead, as discussed in chapter 3, they aggressively disqualify bad-fit opportunities from their pipelines in order to free up time to concentrate on those deals that have a real chance of converting. JOLT sellers go beyond the traditional qualification criteria relating to size, authority, budget, timing, or "fit."

Knowing just how badly high levels of indecision kill deals, JOLT sellers actively monitor for cold feet and aren't afraid to cut bait based purely on signs of customer indecision. This is still only a small percentage of deals (as discussed earlier, perhaps at most 10–15 percent of potential buyers), but the premise is profound: this means a high performer choosing to walk away from a buyer *even if purchase intent is expressed.* Most average-performing sellers would kill for any buyer who goes so far as to say they want to buy the vendor's solution. But the JOLT seller, on gauging high levels of indecision, justifies their time spend accordingly and knows that no amount of product desire can overcome certain levels of buyer indecision. So, instead of pursuing the opportunity with equal time and attention, they are more likely to put it on the back burner or even kill for cause altogether. This is especially important in complex, long-cycle sales. As one leader in the heavy construction company we discussed earlier told us: "In our business, it can take years to close a big deal. Spending that amount of time with an indecisive customer that never closes can end a salesperson's career here."

Complex Selling Behaviors That Increase the Risk of Inaction

This brings us to a second big difference in the outbound sales calls we studied. As outlined previously, outbound selling happens in far more settings than just web conference calls. This is why behaviors such as limiting the exploration take on a different shape in these situations, as the temptation to push boundaries and boil the ocean can be conveyed across months of interactions and through several different communication channels. And, when those live calls do occur—particularly in industries involving any form of technology—the expectation is that some or most of the agenda will be dedicated to a product demonstration: the dreaded demo that buyers love to hate but can't quite seem to quit. And when a seller goes into demo mode, unfortunately too much of JOLT goes out the window.

Why? Well, first, a demo feels more like a presentation than a conversation. Loath to interrupt the flow of a presentation, buyers voice objections at lower rates. But unvoiced objections can translate to unarticulated indecision, reducing instinct to engage in JOLT techniques. This raises the stakes for the seller to actively listen for signs of implicit non-acceptance that can signal indecision lurking below the surface. When we studied demo-centric calls, we found that top sellers were far more likely than average performers to stop their demos to gauge customer reaction to what they're being shown and dig more deeply if they spotted any signs of hesitation, confusion, or uncertainty on the customer's part.

It also turns out that salespeople selling more complex solutions are often guilty of excessive probing and diagnosis. This can come at the expense of a firm recommendation, where the seller decides to continually defer to whatever the customer needs or wants rather than frame it out proactively. As we've discussed at length, though, the buyer racked with indecision fears action, not inaction. Throwing more diagnosis as a way to, in effect, sit on the problem longer is not going to motivate action. The ineffectiveness of this approach can be observed in outbound sales calls in several ways. For instance, it's common for average performers to exhibit probing behavior *more* frequently than their high-performing counterparts. That doesn't mean high performers do not engage in needs diagnosis but instead suggests that they see a time and place for it and avoid doing it excessively, particularly when dealing with highly indecisive customers.

De-risking When an Opt-Out Isn't an Option

Taking risk off the table for a buyer considering a complex solution is just as important as anywhere else, if not more so. Buyers burned by past purchasing mistakes tend to carry a lot of baggage for long periods of time. That baggage comes through in seemingly endless requests for case studies, customer references, and free pilots. While average performers look to fulfill these requests with ROI calculators and whatever collateral they can get their hands on, experienced JOLT sellers instead set clear guidelines during the purchase process as well as realistic expectations about what comes after the purchase, doing so on more than 60 percent of interactions.

The notion of offering downside protection in a complex solution sale feels rather foreign to some sellers and even senior leaders. As we've shared this research with outbound sales teams, the first reaction is to assume this can't be done as part of more complex purchases. The assumptions range from reactions such as "Legal would never allow a money-back guarantee" to "Finance would balk at a backout clause." Still, whenever we raised this question in interviews, experienced sellers start to recall methods they use to de-risk purchase decisions. One common tool is to bolt on a services contract to a product purchase. That feels very counterintuitive because, by definition, adding services to a contract makes the purchase more expensive. You'd think increasing the price tag would increase perceived risk, not decrease it. But JOLT sellers recognize that indecision is rooted in fear of action. Indecision can be a very lonely state for an executive who *wants* to buy, knows the product is needed, and still can't commit. Adding a services element, whereby that supplier is now contractually obligated to be with the buyer in lockstep across portions of the journey, can allay concerns of outcome uncertainty and, ultimately, help the customer to not feel so alone in the decision.

Conclusion

When we split out the outbound sales calls in our study, some interesting differences arose relative to inbound sales channels. For example, salespeople who are pitching more complex solutions to customers on an outbound basis appeared to be more comfortable offering their personal recommendation, as compared to their inbound sales peers. Outbound sellers exhibited this behavior nearly 60–75 percent of the time, versus around 40–50 percent for inbound sellers.

But the differences we found tended to be limited to the relative frequency of specific behaviors, not in their power when it comes to impacting win rates. Why? Because, as we discussed earlier in this chapter, indecision isn't a problem in one go-to-market model or another, it's a human problem. Whether selling in a simple, inbound transactional setting or a complex, long-cycle outbound setting, indecision is something that ensnares a huge number of customers and therefore needs to be managed aggressively by every salesperson, regardless of what they sell and to whom they sell.

In the next chapter, we'll discuss how sales organizations can hire JOLT-ready reps and develop their existing sellers' JOLT skills through purpose-built training and coaching.

CHAPTER ELEVEN

Building the JOLT-Capable Sales Force

A s in most other areas of a company, sales leaders can organize their way out of certain problems. Top-tier opportunities can be handled exclusively by the most tenured sellers.
High-net-worth clients can be routed to the best closers. Accounts
with the greatest growth potential can be managed by key account teams. Smaller, transactional purchases can be handled by
less-experienced teams. These are all problems that, with some
planning and thought, can be worked around by how jobs are
designed, territories are allocated, or hierarchies are placed.

But buyer indecision isn't one of those things that has an easy
org structure solution.

As we've discussed throughout this book, indecision occurs in
moderate or high levels on 87 percent of sales calls. Leaders don't
have the luxury of planning around it, and those who ignore it do

so at their own peril. And the evidence is very clear buyers need the human element that sellers bring to push past their indecision. So, sales leaders looking to improve the ability of their organizations to overcome customer indecision really only have two options to pursue: hiring JOLT-ready reps or developing JOLT skills in their existing sellers.

There's a long-held temptation in sales leadership circles to assume great salespeople are just born with their talent. Some have the "it" factor and some don't. We've certainly heard it voiced many times, having worked with sales teams all over the world. This too was a very common question asked of us after *The Challenger Sale* was published: "Are Challengers born or made?" So, we expect many readers, having reached this point in the book, are wondering the same about JOLT. Can you really replicate JOLT behavior, or is just something that great sellers are born with?

Wondering about the "nature versus nurture" question is completely understandable. Certain humans are born with athletic gifts or musical talent or writing prowess that others can only really dream of. Sales has historically been known to have some undetermined mix of art and science to it. Those subscribing to the "nature" side of this argument might jump straight to hiring, skipping over development on the assumption that it is just too hard or unlikely to succeed. Of course, if hiring is already a need and planned activity, it makes sense to target and screen for people more likely to have JOLT skills. But hiring takes time and decisions are stalling now. Teams can't afford to wait—there is no getting around the hard work of training and coaching existing reps on JOLT skills.

The good news is that JOLT skills are entirely observable and easier to adopt than you might think. We know this in part due to a simple but fundamental fact: people on sales teams right now are *already* demonstrating JOLT behaviors. After all, if they weren't, we wouldn't have found them in our data. We didn't invent JOLT behaviors out of thin air. Instead, we observed high-performing sellers across millions of interactions and many different settings. Most sales leaders we talk to can immediately point out the JOLT sellers on their teams—they've just never thought to look.

However, as we examine JOLT sellers, relative performance often differs by behavior. For example, one sales rep may be world-class at limiting the exploration but struggle a bit more—on a relative basis—with taking risk off the table. Having studied frontline seller behavior for twenty years, we can tell you this is a very common situation when measuring skills. Alternating "sky-lines" fall into place, natural distributions form, and variation often exists at the individual rep level. So even high performers can improve by leaning harder and more often in certain directions. Until we studied sales performance through the lens of buyer indecision, though, we didn't have the means or ability to codify what, specifically, the high performers were doing in these situations. Nor could we understand why it was so necessary.

This last point is incredibly important. There's a purpose and a mission to JOLT behavior. If buyer fear is rooted in deep-seated biases against errors of commission—worry about failure—then anything a rep does to deepen that fear will backfire. As discussed earlier, indecision is solved only when the sales rep properly manages perceived pain—enough to push past inaction, but also enough JOLT to reduce fear of action. As we think about hiring for and developing more JOLT behavior, this teaches us two things.

First, the role of seller is about far more than persuasion. The best JOLT sellers understand their job shifts at some point from one of persuasion to one of motivation. How the salesperson sees themselves and their role in pushing past indecision will present itself clearly in interviews and observation. Second, demonstrating JOLT behavior is as much a seller choice as anything else. Am I increasing or reducing fear? It's a choice made every day, on every deal, and in every conversation. And this lens can be a useful way to evaluate performance.

With that in mind, let's examine in more detail how to approach hiring for JOLT sellers and developing JOLT behaviors across the sales team.

Hiring JOLT Sellers

JOLT skills are no different from other things leaders might hire for, such as business acumen, industry knowledge, or experience selling specific types of products and services. All good hiring processes start with a job profile. But recruiting teams must move from there to begin sourcing candidates and targeting individuals. And trust that there won't be many "I'm good at overcoming indecision" entries on résumés or LinkedIn profiles. So how should companies spot and screen for JOLT skills?

A good first place to start is by pressure testing assumptions about the job profile itself and whether an organization is screening for the right skills and experiences in candidates. In other words, looking at your current JOLT sellers and trying to figure out what experiences or credentials they have in common. But, a word of caution when doing this: hiring managers are human,

and trying to spot patterns in successful, JOLT-capable sellers—
or the opposite, those sellers who struggle to overcome indecision—
can easily lead to confirmation bias. Confirmation bias is the
tendency people have to look for or interpret facts in a way that
supports a preexisting point of view. This bias is ubiquitous in
business, politics, and society in general. Consider, for instance,
the detective who believes a suspect is guilty and overweights
confirmatory evidence while ignoring contradictory evidence.
Confirmation bias can be particularly troublesome when it comes
to creating recruiting profiles. Not only can conventional wisdom
(e.g., "The best sellers are clearly those with prior sales experience" or "Those with industry experience are best-suited to sell to
our customers") seep into hiring decisions, but more nefarious
types of bias can end up driving hiring preference, even if subcon-
sciously (e.g., "One gender is better at sales than another"). Hiring managers need to be especially attuned to what their own
preexisting biases are and let the data speak for itself. Even then,
we recommend that any profiling effort serve only as an input
into the selection process rather than a hard-and-fast arbiter of
who gets an interview (or offer) and who does not.

Early long lists of candidates should have some non-salespeople
as options. Where might those people be found? One company
we work with told us that they found their most JOLT-capable
reps to be individuals with customer success experience. "When
we look at our assessment data, the sellers with the greatest ability
to overcome customer indecision seem to be those who've worked
in our customer success function or came to us with some experience in that area from another organization. We think it's a function of the fact that these folks have the hard job of getting the
customer to adopt our product and embed it in their companies'

workflow, which is ultimately about overcoming their fears about what might go wrong."

It may be that the experience necessary to feel comfortable with JOLT skills—to act as the buying agent for the customer—can come from many different places. One might assume those with a more multidisciplinary background are better positioned to judge indecision levels. Those in your company most familiar with your products might be best positioned to personalize a recommendation. Another sales leader in the software industry told us she has seen an increasing trend to hire away *customers* and convert those people to *sellers*. This was a head-scratcher for us until she explained that "former customers are immediately seen as subject matter experts by prospective customers. They've *done the job* of the person they're selling to and they have personally felt the fear of failure that arises right before a big purchase like the one we're selling." In fact, lots of other professions require motivating others to take action: consultants, teachers, lawyers, and accountants, to name a few.

When considering those with sales experience, there is an added advantage of using past sales performance as at least one indicator of selling in high-indecision moments. After all, a low performer in other settings is not the likeliest candidate to flip a switch and become your best JOLT seller. But not all sales settings are created equal, and evaluating past experience in light of buyer indecision can change how some are viewed. One study participant told us that their assessment was more revealing in terms of patterns to avoid than patterns to hire for: "Our analysis was most revealing in terms of how previous sales experience could be a real swing factor. There are a couple of players in our industry that are known for their hard-charging sales approach and the folks we've hired from those organizations lose far more deals to 'no decision' than reps who've come from other shops."

Interviews remain the primary mechanism most managers use to narrow down potential candidates and select finalists. At a minimum, those interviews should aim to test for and discuss examples involving high buyer indecision. Ask candidates to provide details around their typical approach when a buyer appears to have gotten cold feet in late stages. Prompt them to share stories—from their business or personal lives—about how they motivated somebody else to take action even when that person was indecisive. Or question how they would forecast a deal based on buyer decision dysfunction (readers can download a sample JOLT interview guide from our website, **www.jolteffect.com**).

But it is obviously difficult to mimic buyer emotion within an interview setting. All things equal, better to perform more direct observation of the candidate's ability and willingness to push past moments of indecision. That type of observation used to be much more difficult than it is today. Many sales interactions are recorded and can easily be shared. Privacy concerns may prevent candidate ability to share past interactions with a hiring manager. But interview processes should include simulated conversations or role plays. Progressive organizations are recording those interviews and can then analyze how those candidates handled various indecision situations.

Finalist candidates are commonly asked to complete a prehire survey or diagnostic, testing for specific cognitive abilities or personality traits. Some organizations deploy such assessments far earlier, used as an initial screen before any interview requests are considered. Prehire assessments can be valuable but often are overweighted toward intellectual capacity. Selection decisions for JOLT sellers, however, need also to consider the candidate's emotional quotient. Great JOLT sellers are as conversant in *fears* as they are in *facts*.

Now let's consider how teams should approach developing JOLT behaviors within their existing teams.

Developing JOLT Sellers

Behavior change of any sort is difficult. Our past experience can be an inhibitor, especially when that experience has been informed by weeks or months of sales training and years of observation, trial, and error. And, yes, personality can also influence seller instincts and impact willingness to change. Take limiting the exploration as one example. Some reps may instinctually worry an approach like cooperative overlapping feels rude simply due to their cultural upbringing.

But jolting buyers out of their indecision is just as much about the choices each sales rep makes every day—about how much of their effort is aimed at increasing or reducing buyer fear. It's not that the skills themselves will feel all that foreign. We're all human, after all, and most of us at various points in our personal lives have offered up recommendations to a restaurant or a hit show or any number of products. Any parent can tell you they have limited their own kids' explorations, shutting down lines of questioning before it goes too far. Money-back guarantees and free trials are relatively common offers meant to allay buyer hesitancy.

So, the base JOLT skills will not feel altogether foreign to most people. But to the professional seller they very well might feel highly counterinstinctual. Most teams will have far too many who rely only on increasing buyer fear and overcoming the status quo. It's the tool with which they are most familiar and most comfortable using. That's not an accident. The instinct to relitigate the status quo—over and over again—has been woven into selling orthodoxy for decades. And it is reinforced every day by sales methodologies and training programs. Frontline sales managers also play a large role in driving adherence to processes and practices aimed at helping buyers succeed—supported by layers of ROI calculators, case studies, value stories, and more—rather than helping them avoid failing. At current course and speed, most average-performing salespeople will just keep doing what they've been doing.

The good news is that adopting JOLT does not mean having to throw out your existing sales methodology. No other methodology really addresses overcoming indecision and a buyer's fear of failure. So, if your team loses a lot of deals to inaction, think of JOLT as a booster or overlay to your existing sales methodology, whatever it might be. Adding in JOLT elements won't be duplicative to your current sales method, nor will it be disruptive to the guidance and training already provided to teams. Instead, it becomes a new tool in the seller's toolset—one purpose-built for the part of the sale they've never been taught exists, let alone taught to manage.

But what happens without that JOLT booster? The answer is you can expect to continue losing too many would-be wins, even after you've been selected as the supplier of choice. No sales methodology—no matter how proven—really takes into account the effects of customer indecision. They may deliver fantastic techniques for beating the status quo and showing the customer how they will succeed by pursuing a new way forward, but they overlook the fact that overcoming indecision is less about proving to the customer that they will win than it is about convincing them they won't lose.

What about the role sales managers play in modeling and coaching toward behaviors known to drive success? These are individuals who have risen through the ranks, been promoted, or were hired based in part on their own ability to sell buyers on change. Just like the frontline team, some managers will already be using JOLT skills with regularity. But also like the frontline team—in part because not all of today's sales managers are necessarily strong on JOLT behaviors themselves—there will be plenty of managers who instinctually reinforce a process with a heavy emphasis on overcoming the status quo, dialing up the fear of not purchasing.

It is absolutely critical that sales managers understand why JOLT is so necessary and that they work to drive adoption on an everyday basis. For one, they are often those responsible for rolling up forecasts, best positioned to pressure test levels of indecision early on in deals or observe rep ability in the face of customer indecision. Managers are the last line of defense in ensuring reps are considering decision-making dysfunction when deciding whether to spend time on an opportunity or not. Unfortunately, too often managers will default to spending any coaching time on their best or worst performers, assuming that this is the area from which they can squeeze out the most incremental performance improvement. But indecision will be most vexing and damaging for average performers, who can develop blinders and "happy ears," getting too excited about a buyer who walks in the door seemingly ready to buy. It's up to the sales manager, where appropriate, to tap the brakes and pressure test these deals (see **www .jolteffect.com** for a downloadable set of JOLT coaching questions). Frontline managers also possess the altitude and are often given the authority to get creative on deal terms that may take risk off of the table.

Technology can help managers observe behavior at scale and measure varying levels of JOLT behavior across their teams. One team member may struggle in particular with judging a customer's level of indecision, while another may need more help offering recommendations. Recognizing those differences and tailoring coaching accordingly will help reps make the right choices to JOLT in their next conversation or sales interaction.

Team huddles can help identify new ways of limiting buyer exploration or de-risking decisions. How teams are organized can also speed up idea sharing. For example, T-Mobile finds it useful to organize customer account teams with cross-functional expertise, aligned by city but assigned with a defined set of accounts.[1] But other sales organizations set up regular manager-to-manager idea sessions where coaches can share ideas and observations. Such platforms will undoubtedly help team members ideate new examples of how the best sellers JOLT their way past customer indecision.

Conclusion

Customer indecision cannot be avoided. So, sales leaders must find a way to grow team capability to overcome buyer fear of failure and adopt more JOLT skills. Acquiring those skills via new hires is a viable option, though one that takes time to accomplish and comes with its own set of pitfalls. The vast majority of improvement will come from developing existing sellers, though doing so will require counteracting long-held instincts and assumptions put in place by years of conventional sales training and coaching.

Acknowledgments

Principal Contributors

The research in this book was intensive and relied on contributions from a large team of people at Tethr. Chief among those individuals is the brilliant Tom Shepherd, Tethr's lead data scientist who designed and tested the predictive model that underpinned this entire study. Tom has and continues to build cutting-edge, world-class AI and machine learning models that derive meaning from complex, unstructured conversational data. We were privileged to have worked closely with him for nearly four years and tremendously value his expertise, partnership, and commitment.

We would also like to thank Tethr leaders past and present—especially Mike Mings, Gary Clark, and Robert Beasley—for their partnership and guidance; Gerardo De La O for his analytics expertise and assistance; Adam Larsen, Tethr's CTO, and his team for building the core technology that enabled us to conduct this research; Jon Jobes and his integrations team, with special thanks to Armando Lemus, for help in ingesting the data used in the study; Carl Schultze and Natalia Maher for designing the graphics shown in the book; and Steve Trier and his team of exceptional conversation intelligence experts—most notably, Don Davey, Amanda Lucio, and Kaley Brown—for years of work building the categories and classifiers we used as variables in our model.

With Sincere Thanks

Beyond the principal contributors to this research, there is a long list of individuals and companies without whose commitment and support this book could not have been completed. Thank you in particular to those organizations that contributed their data and provided early feedback on our findings as well as the countless sales reps, managers, and leaders who helped us bring this story to life by sharing their personal tales of customer indecision.

We would also like to thank our business partner, friend, and fellow DCM Insights founding partner, Rory Channer, who added key insight and context based on his many years of experience leading sales and marketing teams.

We had the support of many talented and dedicated professionals who helped guide this book through each phase of the journey: our agent, Jill Marsal of Marsal-Lyon, and the enthusiastic and supportive team at Portfolio, including our editor, Nina Rodriguez-Marty, and our publisher, Adrian Zackheim.

The final thank-you is the most important one. We have been hard at work for nearly two years conducting the research and writing this book. None of this would have been possible without the support, sacrifice, and encouragement from our families.

www.jolteffect.com

NOTES

Preface

1. Neil Rackham, *SPIN Selling* (New York: McGraw Hill, 1988).

Chapter One: The Inaction Paradox

1. Our analysis also reflected the combined effect of multiple, sometimes competing, concepts whose impact changes when paired together (all while still being able to isolate the independent contribution of each variable). This is why the model will, at times, find situations that on the surface may feel counterintuitive. For instance, it's not uncommon for a combination of factors that one would otherwise assume are bad—such as a customer expressing extreme uncertainty—to end up having a positive impact in the model based on the context and surrounding events. So, yes, a potential customer may say a lot of negative things that—if nothing else happened—would likely be a deal killer. But other things do happen, very often involving the other party (in this case the sales rep). How that rep handles that situation has the potential to turn something negative into a positive.

2. William Samuelson and Richard Zeckhauser, "Status Quo Bias in Decision Making," *Journal of Risk and Uncertainty* 1 (1988): 7–59.

3. Jessica Selinger et al., "Humans Can Continuously Optimize Energetic Cost During Walking," *Current Biology* 25, no. 18 (2015): 2452–2456.

4. Daniel Kahneman and Amos Tversky, "The Psychology of Preference," *Scientific American* 246, no. 1 (1982): 160–173.

5. Kahneman and Tversky, "Psychology of Preference." Prospect theory is considered such a central pillar of modern behavioral economics that Kahneman was awarded the Nobel Prize in Economics in 2002 for his work. For more about prospect theory and Kahneman's research into human decision-making see Daniel Kahneman, *Thinking Fast and Slow* (New York: Farrar, Strauss & Giroux, 2013).

6. Daniel Kahneman, "Talks at Google: Thinking Fast and Slow," You-Tube Video, November 10, 2011, https://www.youtube.com/watch?v =CjVQJdIrDJ0.

7. Kahneman and Tversky, "Psychology of Preference."

8. Frederick Leach and Jason Plaks, "Regret for Errors of Commission and Omission in the Distant Term Versus Near Term: The Role of Level of Abstraction," *Personality and Social Psychology Bulletin* 35, no. 2 (February 2009): 221–229.

9. For more on how anticipating future regret from inaction can lead to better personal decisions now see Daniel Pink, *The Power of Regret: How Looking Backward Moves Us Forward* (New York: Riverhead Books, 2022).

10. Ilana Ritov and Jonathan Baron, "Status-Quo and Omission Biases," *Journal of Risk and Uncertainty* 5 (1992): 49–61.

11. Ritov and Baron, "Omission Biases."

12. Veerle Germeijs and Paul de Boeck, "Career Indecision: Three Factors from Decision Theory," *Journal of Vocational Behavior* 62, no. 1 (2003): 11–25; Gordon F. Pitz and Vincent A. Harren, "An Analysis of Career Decision Making from the Point of View of Information Processing and Decision Theory," *Journal of Vocational Behavior* 16, no. 3 (1980): 320–346.

Chapter Three: Judge the Indecision

1. Joseph R. Ferrari, "Christmas and Procrastination: Explaining Lack of Diligence at a 'Real-World' Task Deadline," *Personality and Individual Differences* 14, no. 1 (1993): 25–33; Joseph R. Ferrari and John F. Dovidio, "Examining Behavioral Processes in Indecision: Decisional Procrastination and Decision-Making Style," *Journal of Research in Personality* 34, no. 1 (2000): 127–137.

2. Randy O. Frost and Deanna L. Shows, "The Nature and Measurement of Compulsive Indecisiveness," *Behaviour Research and Therapy* 31, no. 7 (1993): 683–692.

3. Frost and Shows, "Compulsive Indecisiveness."

4. Brent Adamson, Matthew Dixon, and Nick Toman, "The End of Solution Sales," *Harvard Business Review*, July–August 2012.

5. Michel J. Dugas et al., "Intolerance of Uncertainty and Information Processing: Evidence of Biased Recall and Interpretations," *Cognitive Therapy and Research* 29, no. 1 (2005): 57–70.

6. Joseph R. Ferrari and John F. Dovidio, "Behavioral Information Search by Indecisives," *Personality and Individual Differences* 30, no. 7 (2001): 1113–1123.

7. Christopher Anderson, "The Psychology of Doing Nothing: Forms of Decision Avoidance Result from Reason and Emotion," *Psychological Bulletin* 129, no. 1 (2003): 139–167.

8. Anderson, "Doing Nothing."

9. Herbert A. Simon, "Rational Choice and the Structure of the Environment," *Psychological Review* 63, no. 2 (1956): 129–138.

10. Shahram Heshmat, "Satisficing vs. Maximizing: When We Face Too Many Choices, We Can Feel Anxious about Missing Out," Science of Choice (blog), *Psychology Today*, June 13, 2015, https://www.psychology today.com/us/blog/science-choice/201506/satisficing-vs-maximizing.

11. Arne Roets, Barry Schwartz, and Yanjun Guan, "The Tyranny of Choice: A Cross-Cultural Investigation of Maximizing-Satisficing Effects on Well-Being," *Judgment and Decision Making* 7, no. 6 (2012): 689–704; Barry Schwartz et al., "Maximizing Versus Satisficing: Happiness Is a Matter of Choice," *Journal of Personality and Social Psychology* 83, no. 5 (2002): 1178–1197.

12. Eric Rassin, "A Psychological Theory of Indecisiveness," *Netherlands Journal of Psychology* 63, no. 1 (March 2007): 1–11.

13. "Psychology of Procrastination: Why People Put Off Important Tasks Until the Last Minute (Five Questions for Joseph Ferrari, PhD)," American Psychological Association, 2010, https://www.apa.org/news/press /releases/2010/04/procrastination.

14. Joseph R. Ferrari, *Still Procrastinating: The No-Regrets Guide to Getting It Done* (Hoboken, NJ: Wiley, 2010); P. Steel, "The Nature of Procrastination: A Meta-Analytic and Theoretical Review of Quintessential Self-Regulatory Failure," *Psychology Bulletin* 133, no. 1 (2007): 65–94.

15. Rassin, "Indecisiveness."

16. Anderson, "Doing Nothing."
17. Anderson, "Doing Nothing."
18. Rassin, "Indecisiveness."
19. For more on the idea of powerful requests see Matthew Dixon and Brent Adamson, *The Challenger Sale: Taking Control of the Customer Conversation* (New York: Portfolio, 2011). For more on the concept of customer verifiers see Brent Adamson, Matthew Dixon, Nick Toman, and Patrick Spenner, *The Challenger Customer: Selling to the Hidden Influencer Who Can Multiply Your Results* (New York: Portfolio, 2015).
20. Robert Ladouceur et al., "Experimental Manipulations of Responsibility: An Analogue Test for Models of Obsessive-Compulsive Disorder," *Behavioral Research and Therapy* 33, no. 8 (1995): 937–946.

Chapter Four: Offer Your Recommendation

1. Barry Schwartz, "The Paradox of Choice," TEDGlobal 2005, July 2005, https://www.ted.com/talks/barry_schwartz_the_paradox_of_choice?language=en.
2. Sheena S. Iyengar, Wei Jiang, and Gur Huberman, "How Much Choice Is Too Much? Contributions to 401(k) Retirement Plans," Pension Research Council Working Paper 2003-10, Wharton School of Business at the University of Pennsylvania.
3. Iyengar, Jiang, and Huberman, "How Much Choice?" From the authors: "The graph plots the relation between the plan [and] participation rate. Explanatory variables except the number of funds offered are set at their respective mean values and the number of funds offered using a two-stage parametric estimation method. The dotted lines represent the 95 percent confidence intervals."
4. Sheena S. Iyengar and Mark R. Lepper, "When Choice Is Demotivating: Can One Desire Too Much of a Good Thing?," *Journal of Personality and Social Psychology* 79, no. 6 (2000): 995–1006. For more research on how options are both attractive but, at the same time, overwhelming to customers see Leilei Gao and Itamar Simonson, "The Positive Effect of Assortment Size on Purchase Likelihood: The Moderating Influence of Decision Order," *Journal of Consumer Psychology* 26, no. 4 (October 2016): 542–549.

Chapter Five: Limit the Exploration

1. Colin Powell wrote on and spoke about his leadership principles extensively throughout his career. This particular set of quotes comes from his

widely circulated presentation "A Leadership Primer," US Department of the Army, 2006, available at https://www.hsdl.org/?view&did=467329.

2. Creating and leveraging constructive tension is a core skill of Challenger salespeople. For more on this concept see Matthew Dixon and Brent Adamson, *The Challenger Sale: Taking Control of the Customer Conversation* (New York: Portfolio/Penguin, 2011).

3. Kim Scott, *Radical Candor: Be a Kick-Ass Boss without Losing Your Humanity* (New York: St. Martin's Press, 2017).

4. This graphic is a modified version of one that appears in Scott, *Radical Candor*.

5. There have been countless books written on Sakichi Toyoda and his contributions to defining the Toyota manufacturing process. One example is James P. Womack, Daniel T. Jones, and Daniel Roos, *The Machine That Changed the World: The Story of Lean Production* (New York: Free Press, 2007).

6. Kelsey Borresen, "How to Know if You're an Interrupter or a 'Cooperative Overlapper,'" *HuffPost*, March 4, 2021. https://www.huffpost.com /entry/interrupting-or-cooperative-overlapping_l_603e8ae9c5b601179 ec0ff4e.

7. Borresen, "'Cooperative Overlapper.'"

8. Annie Reneau, "A Viral Tik-Tok Video Explains Why Interrupting Others Isn't Always as Rude as It Might Seem," *Upworthy*, February 23, 2021, https://www.upworthy.com/cooperative-overlapping-communication-style.

Chapter Six: Take Risk Off the Table

1. William Payne, *A Practical Discourse of Repentance: Rectifying the Mistakes about It, Especially Such as Lead Either to Despair or Presumption. Perswading and Directing to the True Practice of It, and Demonstrating the Invalidity of a Death-Bed Repentance, 2nd ed.* (London: Samuel Smith and Benjamin Walford, 1695), 557.

2. "Considering OpenOffice? Consider This . . ." (Video). Microsoft. 2010. Archived from the original on January 8, 2018. Retrieved June 17, 2019.

3. Robert Cialdini, *Influence: The Psychology of Persuasion*, revised ed. (New York: Harper Business, 2006). Quote taken from https://www .influenceatwork.com/7-principles-of-persuasion.

Chapter Seven: Becoming a "Buyer's Agent"

1. In August 2018, the industry association representing travel agents renamed itself the American Society of Travel Advisors (ASTA) to reflect

the changing role that these professionals play in helping customers not just book but also plan their travel. In their press release announcing the change, ASTA said, "Travel agents are not just booking agents anymore. They have become trusted Advisors—akin to financial agents and CPAs—who make the overall travel experience better and provide leisure and business travelers maximum value for their travel dollar. What's more exciting is that consumer media and, more important, the traveling public are embracing this shift from agent to an advisor." American Society of Travel Advisors, "American Society of Travel Advisors Unveils New Brand as Travel Advisors," news release, August 28, 2018, https://www.asta.org/About/PressReleaseDetail.cfm?ItemNumber=18306.

2. For more on the similarities between top salespeople and travel agents, see Nick Toman, Brent Adamson, and Cristina Gomez, "B2B Salespeople Need to Act More Like Travel Agents," *Harvard Business Review*, March 7, 2017, https://hbr.org/2017/03/b2b-salespeople-need-to-act-more-like-travel-agents.

3. Kathleen M. Eisenhardt, "Agency Theory: An Assessment and Review," *Academy of Management Review* 14, no. 1 (1989): 57–74.

4. Steven D. Levitt and Stephen J. Dubner, *Freakonomics: A Rogue Economist Explores the Hidden Side of Everything* (New York: William Morrow, 2005).

5. Richard H. Thaler and Cass R. Sunstein, *Nudge: Improving Decisions About Health, Wealth and Happiness* (New Haven: Yale University Press, 2008). For additional research on the two systems of thinking see Daniel Kahneman, *Thinking Fast and Slow* (New York: Farrar, Strauss & Giroux, 2013).

6. James J. Choi et al., "For Better or Worse: Default Effects and 401(k) Savings Behavior," NBER Working Paper No. 8651, December 2001.

Chapter Eight: Beyond Win Rates: JOLT-ing Customer Loyalty

1. Matthew Dixon, Nick Toman, and Richard DeLisi, *The Effortless Experience: Conquering the New Battleground for Customer Loyalty* (New York: Portfolio 2013).

2. Eric Rassin, "A Psychological Theory of Indecisiveness," *Netherlands Journal of Psychology* 63, no. 1 (March 2007): 1–11.

3. Rassin, "Indecisiveness."

4. Eric Rassin et al., "Measuring General Indecisiveness," *Journal of Psychopathology and Behavioral Assessment* 29, no. 1 (2007): 61–68.

5. Randy O. Frost and Kenneth J. Sher, "Checking Behavior in a Threatening Situation," *Behaviour Research and Therapy* 27, no. 4 (1989): 385–389.

6. Rassin, "Indecisiveness."

Chapter Nine: How Much Is Indecision Costing You?

1. Source: Challenger Inc. (unpublished research).

2. Matthew Dixon and Brent Adamson, "The Dirty Secret of Effective Sales Coaching," *Harvard Business Review*, January 31, 2011, https://hbr.org/2011/01/the-dirty-secret-of-effective.

3. In our experience, many out-of-the-box categories offered by conversation intelligence platforms don't deliver out-of-the-box value for practitioners. This is usually because the categories themselves are shoddily constructed and have not been built to generalize across companies and industries—which can result in a high number of false positives and false negatives, bringing into question the validity of the insight itself and ultimately leading to a lot of tuning and rework that customers must take on if they want the insights to hit with any accuracy.

Chapter Eleven: Building the JOLT-Capable Sales Force

1. Matthew Dixon, "Reinventing Customer Service," *Harvard Business Review*, November 1, 2018, https://hbsp.harvard.edu/product/R1806F-PDF-ENG.

INDEX

Page numbers in italics refer to illustrations.

Aberdeen, 168
account management, 146, 186,
     194, 204
action
  and customer regret, 13
  customers fearful of, 14, 190,
     192, 196
  inability to drive it, 171–74
  motivating customers into, 28, 36,
     121, 178, 183, 197, 199–200
  scaring customers into, 26, 30, 38,
     113, 118, 121–22, 128, 185
  See also loss: and inaction vs. action
active listening skills, 36, 96–97,
     104–6, 190
advocacy, 81, *82*, 83, 87
agency dilemmas, 135–40, 143, 188
alternatives, evaluating of, 55–59,
     68, *69*, 70, 73, 86
Amazon, 57–58, 132, 148

ambiguity tolerance, 51, 53–54, *69*,
     70, 90, 188
"analysis paralysis," 53, 90
analyst reports, 21, 54, 136, 180
analytics
  data, xi–xii, 5–7, 31, 139, 176
  sales conversation, xi–xii, 167–77
Anderson, Christopher, 56, 63–64
Apple, 98, 148

B2B
  market, 159
  organizations, 180, 185
  purchases/sales, 15, 122
  software providers, 73
B2C companies, 180
"backtracking" behavior, 54
Baron, Jonathan, 16–17
benefits, capturing of, 18, 20, 30, 37,
     111–12, 117, 127

business deals/decisions
  large, 78, 123, 127, 159, 179,
    187–88
  small, 44, 159–60, 179, 184,
    187, 194
business development reps (BDRs),
  186–87
buyer's agent
  agency dilemma and, 135–40,
    143, 188
  example of, 130–33
  make "yes" easy choice, 140–43
  offer a "default option," 140–42
  role of, 133–35, 143–44, 199
buying process
  and buyer's agent, 133–44
  and customer engagement, 186
  early vs. late stage, 18–19, 23,
    77–78
  the entire process, xiv, 187
  evaluating alternatives and, 55–59
  explanation of, 52, 53–55
  and "satisficers" vs. "maximizers,"
    76–77
  and second guessing, 56, 60,
    73, 127
  and setting outcome expectations,
    191–92

call-auditing tool, 162–63
call centers, 5, 162–65, 167
case studies, 3, 191, 202
CEB, 52–53, 160–61, 183
Challenger Customer, The, xviii–xix
Challenger Sale, The, xiv, xviii,
  100, 195
change
  and action vs. inaction, 17
  customer's aversion to, 3, 10, 22

customers fear of, 178
customers willing to, 201
vs. "pain of the same," xiv, 29
requires effort, 8–9
sales reps sell it, xiv, 8, 178, 203
chief financial officers (CFOs),
  66, 94
choices
  and customer regret, 74, 87
  faced with too many, xvii, 21, 32,
    72–78, 86–87, 131–33
  make people unhappy, 73–77
  "paradox of," 82
  personally advocate for, 81, 82, 83,
    85, 87, 117, 155
  "proactive guidance" and, 80–81
  purposefully minimize them,
    78–79, 81
  and retirement accounts, 74, 75
  the safe one, 187
Christmas shoppers' interviews,
  48–49
churn, 41, 76, 136, 139, 145, 155–56
Cialdini, Robert, 114–15
coaching, 87, 162, 165, 173
  conversation intelligence and,
    167, 170
  of core performers, 160–61
  JOLT questions for, 204
  of JOLT skills, 176, 195–96,
    203–4
  to overcome status quo, xiii, 3
complex solution sales, xviii, 5, 32,
  56, 178–79, 185–87, 189–92
confirmation bias, 198
consumer industries, 179–80
contracts, 76, 118, 160
  carve-outs for, 38, 123–25
  indecision after signing, 151–53

indecision over, 19, 54, 95
and opt-out clauses, 38, 122, 124,
153, 191
for outbound sales, 186
project plans for, 122–23
recanted by customers, 152–53
for service, 192
conversation intelligence
companies of, xii, 5, 104, 169
extract insights from, 168–70, 177
free buyer's guide to, 176
and gauging indecision impact,
167–68, 176
and ineffective action, 168,
171–74, 177
pitfalls of, 168–77
prohibitive cost of, 168, 170,
174–77
conversion rate, 160
average sellers vs. JOLT sellers, 41,
82–83
content of sales calls and, 104,
107, 172–73
and customer indecision, 23–24
high levels of effort and, 154
and inbound sales calls, 182
and narrow set of choices, 79
and sales call objections/rebuttals,
95–96
unbounded research and, 108, *109*
See also win rates
"cooperative overlapping," 7, 105–6,
109, 201
COVID-19 pandemic, xii, 180
CRM data, 159–60, 171, 175
customer acquisition, 145
customer decisiveness, 41, 43, 51
customer disloyalty, 148, 156
Customer Effort Score, 154

customer experience (CX), 146, 157,
167, 171–72, 175–76
customer indecision
assessing, *69*, 70, 176–77
assessing impact of, 158–61
avoid amplifying it, 84–86
effect on win rates, xvii, *24*,
32, 179
hallmark of, 25, 75
high levels of, 22, *23–24*, *40*, 41,
83–84, 151, 189, 194
introduction to, xvi–xx, *4*, 5
personal level of, 48–52, 155
playbook for, xix, 31–33, *34*,
35–42, 48, 156
screening for, 43–45
signs of, 49, 51–52, 58, 62, 68, 71,
96–97, 189
study of, 5–7
testing for early on, 203–4
three drivers of, 17–18, *19*, 20–21
a universal human problem,
70–71, 134, 179, 192–93
will get worse in future, 21–22, 32
See also judging the indecision
customer loyalty
amplifying it, 41, 145
"captive loyalty" and, 150
customer effort and, 153–57
"effort of the experience" and, *147*,
148–50
four flavors of, 146, *147*, 148–51
how to build it, long term,
144–46, 151, 156
and post-decision dysfunction,
151–57
predictors of, 154
and "stickiness" of product/brand,
147, 148–50

customer status quo, 15, 115
   gravitational pull of, 8–11, 26, 33
   introduction to, xiii–xix, 2–3, *4*, 5
   overcoming it, 27–29, 38, 74,
      178, 202–3
   playbook for, xviii–xix, 31–33,
      34, 35
   preference for, *4*, 5, 10–11,
      21–22, *52*
   relitigating it, 25–26, *27*, 28–31,
      40, 114, 117, 154, *155*, 156,
      202–3
   and win rates, *27*
   See also status quo bias
customer success, 53, 91, 146, 172,
      175, 198–99
customer support, 146, 172, 175
customers
   feedback of, 61, 164–67, 176
   need the human element,
      134, 195
   sales reps defer to, 36, 85, 87, 103,
      106, 112, 185, 190
   sales reps' interactions with, 160
   say "no," 161
   say "yes," 140–43, 161
   seeking perfection, 59–61, 70
   sentiments of, 169–70

de Boeck, Paul, 17–18
decision
   avoidance, 62–65, *69*, 70
   importance, 67–70
   mistakes, xvi, 14–17, 21, 28–30,
      33, 38, 133
decision-making approaches
   "compensatory selection," 56–57
   customers worry about, 151–53

and delay tactics, 62–68, *69*, 70
the "maximizers," 59–60, *69*,
      76–77, 119, 126, 146
"noncompensatory selection,"
      56–58
and Powell's formula, 89–90
the "satisficers," 59–60, *69*, 76–77
decision-making dysfunction, 51,
      55–57, 203
"default option," 140–42
delay tactics, 51, 68, 118
   decision avoidance, 62–65, *69*, 70
   information gathering, 47, 89–90
   procrastination, 62–65, *69*, 70
   request more info, 101–3
demos, 59, 61, 74, 99
   denying requests for, 101
   given by sales reps, 94
   indulging requests for, 37
   and lack of information, 20, 47
   negative impact on JOLT, 190
   part of buying process, 53, 186
   repeat requests for, 47, 90
DePaul University, 48
diagnosing needs, xiv, 117
   and complex sales, 190–91
   sales reps rely on, 6, 36, 79,
      87–88, 112
   and win rates, 85, *86*
discounts, 28, 68, 114, 124, 185
Disney, Walt, 146
Dovidio, John, 55

effort
   of the customer, 8–9, 64, *153*,
      154, *155–56*, 157, 183
   of the experience, *147*, 148–50
   and win rates, *153*, 154

Effortless Experience: Conquering the New Battleground for Customer Loyalty, The, 148
emails, 2, 154, 160, 184, 186–87
emotions
    ambiguity tolerance and, 53, 90
    and hiring JOLT-ready reps, 200–201
    markers of, 22–24
    over losing vs. winning, 13
    related to indecision, 22–24, 47–48
    in sales calls, 22–24
    sales reps tap into, 29–30
energy conservation principle, 8–9, 141
engagement styles, 190
    caring personally, 98, *99*, 100, 110
    challenging directly, 98, *99*
    manipulative insincerity, 98, *99*
    model for, 172–74
    obnoxious aggression, *99*, 100
    ruinous empathy, *99*, 100
environmental factors, xvii, 22, 30
    See also sales: environments of

fear
    addressing it, 97, 155
    appealing to, 27, 40
    of failure, 28, 196, 199, 202, 204
    leads to indecision, 17–18, *19*, 20–22, 30, 33–38, 46, 117, 128
    making it worse, 112–18, 128, 155, 185, 196, 202–3
    of not purchasing, xvii, 33
    of purchasing, xvii, 33
    reducing it, 40, 196–97, 201

tapping into, 29–30, 33, 37–38, 40–41
fear, uncertainty, doubt (FUD)
    dialing it up, xv, 26, 30
    four flavors of, 114–17
    history of, 113–14
    inbound sales calls and, 185
    and overcoming uncertainty, 112–17, 118–19
    sellers rely on, 38, 100, 112–13, 118–19, 121–22, 128
Ferrari, Joseph, 48–49, 55, 62
"Five Whys," 101
Freakonomics (Levitt), 136
Frost, Randy, 49–51, 152

Gartner, 52–54, 160–61, 183
Georgetown University, 105
Germeijs, Veerle, 17–18
growth, xix, 14–15, 145–46, 194

Harvard University, 8
Heshmat, Shahram, 59–60
hiring managers, 197–98, 200

IBM, 113, 187
"implicit non-acceptance," 96, 101, 190
inaction
    behaviors that increase it, 189–91
    can be useful, 38
    the cost of, 27, 38
    and customer regret, 13
    customers fearful of, 14
    deals lost to, 2–3, *4*, 5, 11, 31, 159–61, 171, 202
    "inaction inertia," 9
    paradox of, 1–31

inaction (*cont.*)
  recipe for, 23
  root causes of, *4*
  scaring buyers about, 155
  See also loss: from inaction
inbound sales, 5
  auditing calls of, 162–63, 167
  channels of, 179–85
  guiding callers during, 184–85
  high volume of calls for, 180–81
  vs. outbound sales, 192–93
  service requests and, 182–83
  and surveys/interviews, 165
  "time is money," 181–84
  and top sellers, 182–85
indecision sources, 117
  pinpointing them, 45–48
  three primary ones, 18, *19*, 86,
    111, 128
  See also information, lack of;
    outcome uncertainty;
    valuation problems
Indecisiveness Scale, 49–51
*Influence: The Psychology of
  Persuasion* (Cialdini),
  114–15
information, consuming of,
  52–55, 68
information, lack of
  explanation of, 18, *19*, 20–21, 30
  indications of, 46–47
  a main indecision source, 21, 37,
    51, 111, 128
  See also limiting the exploration
information, own the flow of, 37,
  90–94, 108, 155
information, requests for
  acquiesce to, 37, 53, 98, 112
  are revealing, 65

excessive demand for, 19–20, 47,
  90, 137, 155, 191
find root cause of, 101–3, 109
in sales calls, 100
information, search for
  and "analysis paralysis," 53
  in buying process, *52*, 53–55
  by customers, xvii, 21, 60, 112,
    135, 137, 180–81, 188
  discourage customers from, 42
  done after closing, 152
  fear over not enough, 18, 21,
    132–33, 141
  and impact on win rates, 108, *109*
  See also limiting the exploration
insurance industry, 77–78, 138
internet, 130–33, 149–50, 180–81
interviews
  for hiring JOLT-ready reps,
    200–201
  JOLT interview guide for, 200
Iyengar, Sheena, 78–79

"jelly" experiment, 78–79
job profile, 197–98
JOLT method
  assessing for organizations,
    176–77
  in different sales environments,
    178–93
  easier sales experience and,
    155–57
  four techniques for, xix, 35–42
  how to apply them, 39–42
  introduction to, xiii–xx
  payoffs of, 39, *40*, 41–42
  reduces post-decision dysfunction,
    153–57
  and win rates, 39, *40*, 41

See also judging the indecision;
limiting the exploration; take
risk off the table
JOLT sellers
assessing skills of, 162–77, 204
hiring them, 162, 195–201, 204–5
specific skills of, 182–85, 188–91,
195–98, 201–5
train current reps as, 162, 195–97,
201–5
judging the indecision, 199
ambiguity tolerance, 51, 53–54,
69, 70, 188
consuming of information,
51–55, 68
content with "good enough,"
59–62, 68, 70
customer delay tactics, 62–68
customers seek perfection,
59–61, 70
and decision importance, 67–70
evaluating alternatives and, *52*,
55–59, 68, *69*, 70, 73, 86
explanation of, 35–36, 38–39,
41, 45
a four-step process, 51–71
and personal level of indecision,
48–52
and pinpointing indecision, 45–48
procrastination vs. decision
avoidance, 62–65, *69*, 70
the "satisficers" vs. "maximizers,"
59–60, *69*, 76–77
scorecard for, 68, *69*
and screening customers, 43–45
and time pressure, 67–70
top sellers excel at, 182–83

Kahneman, Daniel, 11–13

Ladouceur, Robert, 67
"lead steer effect," xviii
Lepper, Mark, 78–79
Levitt, Steven, 136
limited-time offers, 68, 114–15
limiting the exploration, 188,
196, 201
anticipate needs/objections, 37, 90,
95, *96*, 97–98, 108–9
on expert sales calls, 103–10, 184
explanation of, 36–39, 41,
117–18, 128
find roots of info request,
101–3, 109
and outbound sales, 189–90
own the flow of info, 37, 90–94,
108, 155
practice radical candor, 37, 98, *99*,
100–103, 109
and source of indecision, 48, 117
and subject matter experts,
91–93, 108
three skills for, 90, 95, 98, 108–9
using Powell's formula, 89–90
and win rates, *109*
See also engagement styles; sales
calls/conversations
listening skills. *See* active listening
skills
loss
and avoiding mistakes, 14–17, 21,
27–28, 31, 77–78, 128
customers fearful of, 41, 112,
116, 118
errors of commission and,
13–17, 77
errors of omission and, 13–17,
77, 196
from inaction, 27–28, 77, 159–60

loss (*cont.*)
   and inaction vs. action, 14–17,
      27–28, 31, 37
   personally responsible for, 15,
      78, 127
   See also omission bias
"loss aversion" concept, 11–14,
      77–78, 128
"lost to inaction" rate, 159–60

machine learning, xi, xix, 1, 5–7,
      167, 169
Magic Quadrant, 54, 112
medical profession, 43–44, 73
Microsoft, 113–14
money-back guarantees, 121–22,
      185, 191, 201

"need to think about it" phrase,
      24–25, 86, 111–12, 126
Net Promoter Scores, 154, 172
Nudge: Improving Decisions about
      Health, Wealth, and
      Happiness (Thaler and
      Sunstein), 140–41

objections
   anticipating them, 37, 81, 90,
      95–97, 108–9
   damaging impact of, 23, 190
   and demos, 190
   find root cause of, 101–3
   how to handle them, xiii
   offering rebuttals to, 95,
      96, 97
   stated, 95, *96*
   unstated, 37, 97
   and win rates, 95, *96*, 97

offer your recommendation, 48,
      184, 190, 201
   to avoid amplifying indecision,
      84–86
   and diagnosing needs, 79, 85,
      86, 117
   explanation of, 36–39,
      41, 117, 128
   as personal advocate, 81, *82*, 83,
      85, 87, 117, 155
   as proactive guidance, 79, *80*,
      81, *82–84*, 87, 102–3, 109,
      125–26
   too many choices and, 72–78,
      86–87
   two skills needed for, 79–84
   and win rates, *80*, *82–83*, 85
omission bias, xvi, 11, 13–17,
      29, 30
online purchases, 130–31,
      180–81, 184
opportunities
   deprioritizing them, 59, 67–69, 71
   disqualifying them, 22, 35–36, 68,
      69, 70–71, 128, 188–89
   "kill for cause," 2, 64, 189
   qualifying them, 35, 43–45, 69
   scorecard for, *69*, 70
Othello (Shakespeare), 113
outbound sales
   auditing calls of, 163
   buyers for, 186–87
   channels of, 185–89
   complex solution, 5, 185–86,
      189–92
   and excessive probing/diagnosis,
      190–91
   vs. inbound sales, 192–93

and limiting the exploration, 189–90

long-cycle sales and, 187–90

offer downside protection in, 191–92

risk of inaction and, 189–91

and surveys/interviews, 165

outcome uncertainty

allay fears of, 192

explanation of, 18, *19*, 20–21, 30, 128

and FUD, 38, 112–17, 118–19

hardest to overcome, 111–12, 127–28

indications of, 46–48, 90

and large businesses, 188

offer confidence givers, 121–25, 128

offer risk protection, 38, 121–24, *125*, 128

and setting outcome expectations, 119, *120*, 146

and starting small, 38, 125–27, 138

take risk off the table, 37–38

tools for overcoming it, 185

and win rates, *125*, 128

See also take risk off the table

"pain of the same," xiv, 28, 33, 38, 115–16

Paradox of Choice: Why More Is Less, The (Schwartz), 72

Payne, William, 113

performance evaluations, 7, 162–67, 196–97, 199–200

pilots, xiv, 20, 44, 53–54, 59, 61, 191

post-decision dysfunction, 71, 82

explanation of, 41, 151, 156

JOLT method reduces it, 41, 153–57

types of, 75–76, 151–53

post-sale

behavior, *52*

churn, 41, 76, 136, 139, 145, 155–56

customer disloyalty, 148, 156

re-setting of expectations, 146

surveys/interviews, 162, 165–67

Powell, Colin, 89–90

pressure-selling tactics, 68, 114–15

See also fear, uncertainty, doubt (FUD)

pressure testing, 197, 203–4

principal-agent problem, 135–40, 143, 188

proactive guidance, 79, *80*, 81, *82–84*, 87, 102–3, 109, 125–26

procrastination, 62–65, *69*, 70, 90

productivity, 14–15, 32, 119, 159–60, 182

professional services support, 19, 38, 57, 123, 170, 173, 175, 188

project plans, 122–23

proof-of-concept trials, xiv, 2, 20, 59, 61

proof points, xiii, 3, 112

prospect theory, 11, *12*, 13, 77

purchase

de-risking, 117–27, 155–56, 191–92, 204

decision, 16, 32, 45, *52*

delays, 49, 62–67

See also delay tactics

purchase intent, 29, 33, 65, 161
  FUD and, 115
  impact of indecision on, 23–25
  inbound sales calls and, 181, 183
  JOLT sellers and, 34,
    133–34, 189
  and outbound sales calls, 186
  and relitigating status quo,
    26, 155
  and "satisficers" vs.
    "maximizers," 76
purchasing consultants, 20,
  136, 152

quality assurance (QA) teams,
  162–65

Rackham, Neil, xi, xviii
radical candor, 37, 98, *99*,
  100–103, 109
Rassin, Eric, 63–64, 151–53
realtors, 136
recording platforms, xii, 5, 167
  See also Teams; Webex; Zoom
reference calls, 20, 37, 44–45, 47,
  53, 90, 99, 102, 112, 191
regret, 16, 112
  ambiguity tolerance and, 53
  over action vs. inaction, 13
  over purchases, 24, 41, 87
  too many choices and, 74, 82,
    87, 133
request for proposal (RFP), 56–58
research. *See* information, search for
retirement accounts, 74, *75*
return on investment (ROI), xiii, 2,
  3, 26, 28, 47, 112, 119, 168,
  191, 202
revenue generation, 41

reviews
  customer, xiii, 20–21, 53, 112,
    136, 152, 180
  pipeline, 1–3, 43
risk. *See* take risk off the table
Ritov, Ilana, 16–17
Roets, Arne, 60

SaaS company/market, 101, 159
safety net, 42, 121, 155–56
sales
  cancellation of, 121–22, 124,
    152–53, 185
  closing of, 7, 34, 45, 64, 71, *96*,
    106, 117, 159–60, 185
  common themes among, 179
  cycles of, 7, 159–60, 163
  and definition of success, 127
  early stage vs. back half, 77–78
  effectiveness, 32–33, *34*, 161, 167,
    171, 178
  the enemy in, 3–5
  environments of, xvii, 178–92
  impact of indecision on, xix, *4*,
    22–23, *24*, 25–27
  long-cycle, 187–90
  and main point of contact, 61
  by selling less up front, 38, 126–27

sales calls/conversations
  active engagement in, 106, 109–10
  and agency dilemma, 138
  and asking for the sale, 140, 142–43
  auditing them, 162–67, 174,
    176–77
  "cooperative overlapping" in, 7,
    105–6, 109, 201
  and deferring to customers, 36, 85,
    87, 103, 106, 112

demo-centric, 190
detect indecision in, *4*, 5, 18, *19*,
    20–22, *23*, 49, 51
interrupting during, 7, 104,
    105, 106
JOLT skills used in, 39–40
objections during, 95
and proactive guidance/advocacy,
    82–83
purposeful silence in, 7, 106, *107*,
    108–9
recorded, 5, 154, 162,
    167–68, 200
sales rep talk time in, 7, 103, *104*
studies of, xi–xii, xviii–xix, 1–7
of top sellers, 103, *104–5*, 106,
    107, 108–10, 143–44
See also active listening skills;
    limiting the exploration
sales managers, 64, 68
audit sales calls, 162–67
coaching efforts of, 160–62,
    165, 203–4
focus on best/worst performers,
    203–4
must drive JOLT adoption, 203–4
playbook for, 157
use surveys/interviews, 166
sales methods
and customer indecision, 27,
    202–3
let customers wallow, 115–16
make customers feel isolated, 116
pressure-selling, 68, 114–15
scarcity, 114–15, 185
urgency, 114, 185
sales organizations, xiii, xviii, xx, 1,
    3, 151, 156
assess indecision, 158–66

assess sellers' JOLT skills, 162–77
impact of indecision on, 32
"lost to inaction" rate of, 159–60
share/teach JOLT knowledge, 204
use conversation analytics, 167–68
use surveys/interviews, 165–66
sales process, xiv, 7, 19, 23, 34–35,
    45, *52*, 171
sales reps
admit not having answer,
    139–40, 144
ask for the business/the sale, 140,
    142–43
attuned to indecision, 34–35
bridge intent and action gap, 34,
    45, 161
can make indecision worse, 25–33,
    38, 45, 68
compensation of, 121–22
default playbook for, xvii–xix, 25
effect of indecision on, 161
give competitor feedback,
    138–39, 143
hold the balance of power, 136–37
instill confidence, 41, 119, 121,
    128, 134, 142
interactions with customers, 160
"nature versus nurture" and, 195
outcome-driven, 151
reactive vs. proactive, 79–80, 85
role/job of, 31, 133–34, 178,
    183, 197
as trusted advisor, 37, 44–45, 91,
    134, 137, 140, 184, 195
and win rates, *104–5*, 107, 161
See also buyer's agent
Samuelson, William, 8
Schwartz, Barry, 72–77, 82
scorecards, 68, *69*, 164

Scott, Kim, 98–101
Selinger, Jessica, 9
Shakespeare, 113
Sher, Kenneth, 152
Shows, Deanna, 49–51
SMB segment, 159
software, 10, 14–15, 74, 119,
    138, 199
  automatic speech recognition, xii,
    5, 167
  costs, 174
  and FUD-based messages, 113–14
  natural language processing, 5, 22
  vendors, 73, 170
solutions engineers, 47, 53, 91,
    94, 108
SPIN Selling (Rackham), xi, xviii
start-ups, 21, 32, 54
status quo bias, xvi, 8–11, 16–17
  See also customer status quo
subject matter experts, 47, 53, 133
  consulted after decision, 152
  customers hired as, 199
  lack of, 184
  others brought in as, 91–93, 108
  sales reps as, 37, 81, 91–94,
    103–8, 134–35, 139, 142–43
Sunstein, Cass, 140–41
surveys, 162, 165–67, 176, 200

take risk off the table, xiv, 48,
    196, 204
  de-risk the purchase, 117–27,
    155–56, 191–92, 204
  explanation of, 37–39, 41,
    119, 128
  for individual buyers, 184, 187
  offer confidence givers,
    121–25, 128

offer risk protection, 38, 121–24,
    125, 128, 169, 192–92
  set outcome expectations, 119,
    120, 156, 169, 191–92
  and starting small, 38, 125–27, 138
  and using FUD, 112–19
  win rates and, *120*, 128, *129*
Tannen, Deborah, 105
Teams, xii, 5, 167
technology, 93–94, 167–68, 170,
    176–77, 190, 204
Tethr, xii, 5–7, 154, 167–69
Tethr Effort Index (TEI), 154
Thaler, Richard, 140–41
thinking systems
  "Automatic System," 140–41
  "Reflective System," 140–41
time
  is money, 181–83
  is scarce resource, xiv, 69, 182, 184
  pressure, 63, 67–70
transactional sales, 5, 32, 95, 121,
    138, 178–80, 185, 192, 194
travel agents/advisors, 130–33, 181
trust, 118
  breaking it, 116
  building of, xiv, 37, 137–40,
    143, 146
  influences on, 184
  lack of, 137
  in seller's expertise, 81, 135,
    141–42
  and win rates, 134–35
  See also sales reps: as trusted advisor
Tversky, Amos, 11–13

valuation problems
  and excessive choice, 78, 86
  explanation of, 17–18, *19*, 21, 30

indications of, 46
and large businesses, 188
a main indecision source, 111, 128
offer recommendations for, 36,
87–88, 184
and proactive guidance/advocacy,
81–82
Vanguard, 74–75
virtual sales, xii
vision, agreement to, 28, 33, *34*, 35,
38, 45, 133

wealth management industry,
126–27
Webex, xii, 5, 167
win rates
and building trust, 134–35
and customer effort, *153*, 154
and customer objections, 95,
96, 97

and de-risking skills, 128, *129*
effect of indecision on, xvii, *24*,
32, 179
with JOLT method, 39, *40*, 41
limiting the exploration and, *109*
"proactive guidance" and, *80*
"recommend skills" and, *82–83*, 85
relitigating status quo and, *27*
risk protection and, *125*, 128
and sales effectiveness, 161
and sales rep interruptions, *105*
and sales rep silence time, 107
and sales rep talk time, *104*
setting outcome expectations
and, *120*
www.jolteffect.com, 68, 162–63,
165, 200

Zeckhauser, Richard, 8
Zoom, xii, 5, 167